Automating Workflows with GitHub Actions

Automate software development workflows
and seamlessly deploy your applications using
GitHub Actions

Priscila Heller

BIRMINGHAM—MUMBAI

Automating Workflows with GitHub Actions

Group Product Manager: Wilson D'souza

Publishing Product Manager: Shrilekha Inani

Senior Editor: Shazeen Iqbal

Content Development Editor: Rafiaa Khan

Technical Editor: Nithik Cheruvakodan

Copy Editor: Safis Editing

Project Coordinator: Shagun Saini

Proofreader: Safis Editing

Indexer: Rekha Nair

Production Designer: Jyoti Chauhan

First published: August 2021

Production reference:1110821

Published by Packt Publishing Ltd.

Livery Place

35 Livery Street

Birmingham

B3 2PB, UK.

ISBN 978-1-80056-040-6

www.packt.com

My special thanks and endless admiration to my husband, Dr. Michael Devin Heller, who supported me when I was writing my very first book during times that were trying in more ways than I could have predicted. To my mom and my brother, who cheered me on across the globe, my love and gratitude. My appreciation and many thanks to the Packt team, especially to Shazeen Iqbal, Sankalp Khattri, and Neil D'mello who believed in my potential before I did.

To my dad, who always invested in my education and development: I wish you were here.

– Priscila Heller

Contributors

About the author

Priscila Heller was born and raised in Brazil, where she obtained a bachelor's degree in journalism. She moved to the United States in 2011, where she has been living ever since. After working in many different fields, she found a career opportunity in tech and went back to school to pursue a degree in information system technology. In 2016, Priscila joined GitHub as an enterprise support agent. Over the years, she has been promoted a few times, and today she is a senior manager of Premium Support.

Priscila believes in the power of technology, education, and communication. She considers the democratization of knowledge and information to be invaluable for the cultural, social, economic, and scientific development of society and humanity.

About the reviewer

Melanie Cooper is a lifelong techie, and career tech professional, having spent the last few years as an engineer at GitHub assisting administrators and developers with the configuration and management of their GitHub enterprise solutions, with a specialization in Actions and Packages. A North Carolina native, she resides in Raleigh with her husband, along with their two dogs, and four cats. She is also a strong supporter and an avid investor in cryptocurrency– currently focusing work and contributions toward charitable causes such as $FEG (Feed Every Gorilla), a community that helps fund saving the lives of primates in Africa.

Table of Contents

Section 2: Advanced Concepts and Hands-On Exercises to Create Actions

3
A Closer Look at Workflows

4
Working with Self-Hosted Runners

5

Writing Your Own Actions

6

Marketplace – Finding Existing Actions and Publishing Your Own

Section 3: Customizing Existing Actions, Migrations, and the Future of GitHub Actions

7
Migrations

8
Contributing to the Community and Finding Help

9
The Future of GitHub Actions

Preface

GitHub Actions is an elegant solution to help anyone involved in the software development lifecycle automate everyday tasks and use their resources more efficiently.

This is the ultimate guide to accompany you on your journey of learning about and applying the benefits of keeping your code and automation pipelines in one single place. By the end of this book, you will have all the knowledge you need to implement CI/CD using GitHub Actions.

Who this book is for

This book was specially written for beginner users of GitHub and GitHub Actions in general.

This book is also for anyone who is involved in the software development lifecycle, for readers who are curious about what GitHub Actions is, and what can be accomplished with it, and for anyone who wants to learn a new skill that will help their career in software development.

What this book covers

Chapter 1, Learning the Foundations of GitHub Actions, introduces GitHub, YAML, and other concepts that are the foundation of GitHub Actions.

Chapter 2, Deep-Diving into GitHub Actions, presents specific concepts, components, and characteristics of GitHub Actions in more detail.

Chapter 3, A Closer Look at Workflows, presents in-depth information about workflows, the core of GitHub Actions. This chapter includes several real-life examples.

Chapter 4, Working with Self-Hosted Runners, gives an overview of what self-hosted runners are, how to create an environment to host runners, and creating a workflow that uses a self-hosted runner.

Chapter 5, Writing Your Own Actions, guides you on creating actions of all three kinds: Docker, JavaScript, and composite run steps.

Chapter 6, Marketplace: Finding Existing Actions and Publishing Your Own, guides you on how to find existing actions that were created by the GitHub Actions community, and how to publish actions that you create.

Chapter 7, Migrations, looks at how to migrate from other CI/CD platforms such as Azure Pipelines, GitLab CI/CD, and Jenkins into GitHub Actions.

Chapter 8, Contributing to the Community and Finding Help, covers how you can participate in the GitHub Actions community to both ask for and offer help.

Chapter 9, The Future of GitHub Actions, takes a look at the public GitHub roadmap and highlights GitHub Actions features that will be added in the future.

To get the most out of this book

This book is a comprehensive guide that will help you learn about GitHub, YAML, and GitHub Actions from scratch. The only expectation is that you have general knowledge of navigating the internet.

Software/hardware covered in the book	OS requirements
YAML	Windows, macOS, and Linux (any)
GitHub	Windows, macOS, and Linux (any)
Git	Windows, macOS, and Linux (any)
JavaScript	Windows, macOS, and Linux (any)
Docker	Windows, macOS, and Linux (any)
Azure Pipelines	Windows, macOS, and Linux (any)
Jenkins	Windows, macOS, and Linux (any)
GitLab CI/CD	Windows, macOS, and Linux (any)

If you are using the digital version of this book, we advise you to type the code yourself or access the code via the GitHub repository (link available in the next section). Doing so will help you avoid any potential errors related to the copying and pasting of code.

For some chapters, you will need to clone the following GitHub repository to proceed with the exercises:

`https://github.com/PacktPublishing/Automating-Workflows-with-GitHub-Actions`

Download the color images

We also provide a PDF file that has color images of the screenshots/diagrams used in this book. You can download it here: `http://www.packtpub.com/sites/default/files/downloads/9781800560406_ColorImages.pdf`.

Conventions used

There are a number of text conventions used throughout this book.

`Code in text`: Indicates code words in text, database table names, folder names, filenames, file extensions, pathnames, dummy URLs, user input, and Twitter handles. Here is an example: "Mount the downloaded `WebStorm-10*.dmg` disk image file as another disk in your system."

A block of code is set as follows:

```
jobs:
  build:
    runs-on: ubuntu-latest
    steps:
    - name: Close Issue
```

Any command-line input or output is written as follows:

```
$ ls -al ~/.ssh
```

Bold: Indicates a new term, an important word, or words that you see onscreen. For example, words in menus or dialog boxes appear in the text like this. Here is an example: "Select **System info** from the **Administration** panel."

> Tips or important notes
> Appear like this.

Get in touch

Feedback from our readers is always welcome.

General feedback: If you have questions about any aspect of this book, mention the book title in the subject of your message and email us at customercare@packtpub.com.

Errata: Although we have taken every care to ensure the accuracy of our content, mistakes do happen. If you have found a mistake in this book, we would be grateful if you would report this to us. Please visit www.packtpub.com/support/errata, selecting your book, clicking on the Errata Submission Form link, and entering the details.

Piracy: If you come across any illegal copies of our works in any form on the Internet, we would be grateful if you would provide us with the location address or website name. Please contact us at copyright@packt.com with a link to the material.

If you are interested in becoming an author: If there is a topic that you have expertise in and you are interested in either writing or contributing to a book, please visit authors.packtpub.com.

Share Your Thoughts

Once you've read *Automating Workflows with GitHub Actions*, we'd love to hear your thoughts! Scan the QR code below to go straight to the Amazon review page for this book and share your feedback.

https://packt.link/r/1800560400

Your review is important to us and the tech community and will help us make sure we're delivering excellent quality content.

Section 1: Introduction and Overview of Technologies Used with GitHub Actions

In this section, you will get a basic understanding of the technologies that make using GitHub Actions possible. An overview of what **Continuous Integration/Continuous Deployment (CI/CD)** is will also be included.

The following chapters will be covered in this section:

- *Chapter 1, Learning the Foundations for GitHub Actions*
- *Chapter 2, Deep-Diving into GitHub Actions*

1
Learning the Foundations for GitHub Actions

Independently of your current level of expertise, by the time you have finished reading the last chapter in this book, you will have completed all the steps needed to implement a cohesive **Continuous Integration/Continuous Delivery (CI/CD)** workflow using **GitHub Actions**. You will also have familiarity with many other systems and practices that have helped GitHub Actions gain popularity in the software development and **DevOps** world.

Automation is the heart of most modern DevOps practices. Many tools have been created to allow for automated tests, builds, and deployment, and GitHub Actions is one of those tools. It is an elegant solution that offers the convenience of creating and managing CI and CD workflows from GitHub, the largest code-hosting platform in the world.

It is important to understand the basic concepts of CI and CD before creating and managing GitHub Actions workflows. It is also relevant to learn about some of the technologies that make GitHub Actions possible, such as GitHub—the platform where all GitHub Actions live— and **YAML Ain't Markup Language**, commonly known as **YAML**—the markup language that powers GitHub Actions workflows. In this chapter, you will learn more about the following topics:

- Understanding the basics of CI/CD

- Introduction to GitHub: creating a user account

- Discovering the basics of Git and GitHub

- Introducing YAML

Technical requirements

In this introductory chapter, you will create a GitHub account and a GitHub repository and will review a YAML file, as hands-on practice in preparation for the subsequent chapters in this book. To accomplish all that, you will need the following:

- A computer or laptop with access to the internet, and modern browsers, such as the latest versions of **Safari**, **Firefox**, **Chrome**, and **Microsoft Edge**.

- A **command-line utility**: For macOS and Linux, you will need a system such as **Terminal**, where you can run shell and `Git` commands. For Windows, you will need to download and install **Git Bash**, if you do not already have it installed.

- An email address, which you will need in order to create a GitHub account.

- A text editor such as **Atom**, **Visual Studio Code** (**VS Code**), **Sublime**, and so on.

Understanding the basics of CI/CD

Before jumping into the core concepts of CI and CD, it is helpful to understand more about the history and evolution of the **software development life cycle**. While this section will not present a comprehensive list of all software development methods that may have led to the progress and adoption of CI and CD practices, it will present relevant concepts that will help illustrate why CI and CD are widely adopted today.

A brief trip through the history of software development

Many believe that software engineering dates back to the **1960s**. During that time, software engineering and computing in general were costly, which likely nudged software engineers into practicing software development in a similar way to how hardware production was done. In other words, software development started as a slow, cautious, and methodical practice that followed a sequence of steps aimed at delivering perfect products. This method is known currently as the **Waterfall** model, which is composed of seven phases, each of which depends on the successful and sequential completion of the previous phase. The Waterfall model is known for its inflexible, process-oriented, and sequential nature.

Over time, many issues surfaced in the Waterfall model. For example, **extensive** and **time-consuming** planning and approvals were needed before software engineers even had the chance to start writing code. By the time software was written, tested, and deployed, months had passed and customers' needs had changed completely. The Waterfall model did not allow for many iterations, and when changes were needed, this was a long and expensive process that often created bottlenecks and resulted in obsolete or unused features.

While the Waterfall model was predominant between the 1960s and **1980s**, there was an awareness that a fast, flexible, lightweight, product-focused, and people-focused—as opposed to process-focused—approach was needed.

In the early 1990s, **Extreme Programming** (**XP**) reinforced the concept that tests should be written to describe how code should work, which was also the center of **test-driven development** (**TDD**) practices. The XP community then announced a practice that later would help shape what is today known as CI. They announced the use of automated processes to frequently integrate all code across developing teams, with the intention of delivering code that could be sent to production at any given time. This practice has resulted in many builds per day, which improves the predictability and efficiency of the software development life cycle and allows for constant interaction with customers to satisfy their ever-changing needs. This process, in conjunction with other philosophies and software development methods that were gaining traction in the 1990s, later formed the **Agile Manifesto**.

Many similar software development practices emerged between the 1990s and early 2000s. A group of 17 independent thinkers representing **XP**, **Scrum**, **Adaptive Software Development** (**ASD**), and other communities met to find their commonalities in approaches, as well as to try to find a different approach to heavyweight software development practices.

The Agile Manifesto was created at the end of that meeting when, among all the different software development practices, the **Agile Alliance** was formed.

Agile encompasses many practices that are lightweight, code- and people-oriented, and highly adaptive. Other modern approaches, some of which predate Agile, are also based on the idea that the software development cycle should be highly adaptive and built frequently. Based on these premises, CI and CD have gained more space among software developers across the globe.

The main idea behind CI is that automated processes should be in place to test and build software many times a day. This is important because bugs are commonly introduced at the intersection or integration of two different pieces of code. In other words, CI practices manage processes, which allows software engineers to focus on the code itself.

CD follows in the footsteps of CI. It focuses on gathering all changes to code—such as new features, bug fixes, and configuration changes—and sending them to users—or production—as safely, sustainably, and quickly as possible.

CI in conjunction with CD can be both powerful and challenging, given the shift in culture that must accompany the adoption of these practices. When combined and adopted across a company, they can help ensure high-quality, lightweight, and adaptive software development.

Many tools have been created to help software and operations engineers build a CI/CD pipeline. GitHub Actions is arguably the most popular one: it makes it easier to automate the building, testing, and deployment of code on any platform—including Linux, macOS, and Windows—without leaving the repository where the code lives. All of this can happen while GitHub manages the execution and provides rich feedback and security for every step in your workflow.

Because GitHub Actions happen within a repository hosted on GitHub, a GitHub account is needed. Basic knowledge of GitHub as a platform is also helpful. In the next section, you will learn how to create a GitHub account, as well as how to use some basic Git and GitHub features.

Introduction to GitHub: creating a user account

GitHub is the largest code-hosting platform in the world. It uses Git as version control, and most activities happen on a repository hosted on GitHub. This and other features such as **pull requests**, **project boards**, and GitHub Actions allow software engineers, operations engineers, product managers, and everybody else involved in software development to collaborate in one place.

To start hosting code on GitHub, a user account is needed. Different accounts can be created on GitHub. While some account types are paid for, such as *Team* and *Enterprise* accounts, it is also possible to create a free user account. You can learn about all the different account types offered by GitHub, as well as the features offered with each account, by accessing `https://docs.github.com/en/free-pro-team@ latest/github/getting-started-with-github/types-of-github- accounts`.

While the GitHub *Free* account type will be used throughout this book, learning about the features offered in other account types may help you choose an account that is appropriate for the scope of your project.

In the next few sections, you will learn how to create a free user account, as well as set up authentication options such as **personal access tokens** (**PATs**) and a **Secure Shell (SSH)** key.

Creating a free user account on GitHub

If you already have a GitHub account, you will not need to follow the steps in this section.

When you create a personal user account on GitHub, you have access to features such as unlimited public and private repositories and 2,000 actions minutes per month. After you create a user account, you can use a few different authentication methods to retrieve data related to your account and its resources, outlined as follows:

- On the web browser, you can provide your username and password.
- On the **application programming interface** (**API**), you can use a PAT.
- On the command line, you can use an SSH key.

The next steps will show you how to create a GitHub Free user account. You will also learn how to generate a PAT and an SSH key that will be used in upcoming sections and chapters.

To sign up for a GitHub Free personal user account, follow these steps:

1. Navigate to `https://github.com/join`.

2. Fill in the blank fields with your information. Note that you will need to choose a unique username. An existing email address will also be needed, as well as a password.

3. Solve the verification puzzle and click **Verify**. Then, click on **Create account**.

4. Follow the prompts on the next page and click **Complete setup**. An email will be sent to the email address you provided in *Step 2*.

5. The next screen will ask you to verify your email address. Although the account creation does not depend on having your email verified, you will not be able to use certain features—such as GitHub Actions—without a verified email address. For this reason, verifying your email address is required for the scope of this book.

6. Open your email account. You should see an email that looks like this:

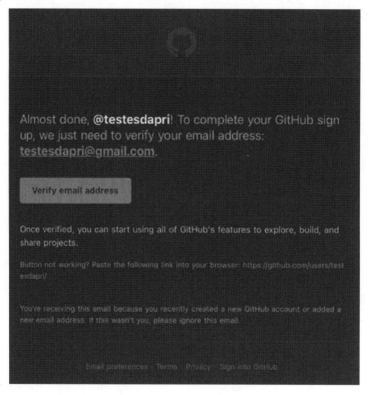

Figure 1.1 – An example of the email sent by GitHub requesting you to verify your email address

7. Click on **Verify email address**.

Great job! Your personal user account has been created on GitHub, and you should be able to find it by navigating to `https://github.com/your-username`, where *your-username* is the unique username that you chose in *Step 2*.

Creating a PAT

Many popular GitHub Actions workflows use a **PAT** or an **SSH key**. This section will walk you through the creation of a PAT, in preparation for future chapters where one will be needed.

A PAT is a string of characters that can be used in place of a password against the GitHub API and on the command line. Different scopes can be attributed to a PAT to specify exactly what level of access is needed. Scopes are often chosen to limit access: nothing beyond the selected scopes can be accessed.

The next steps will guide you in creating a PAT with the `repo`, `user`, and `workflow` scopes. Understanding all the available scopes on GitHub is not part of what will be covered in this book. However, it is helpful to learn what kinds of access each scope grants. To learn more, see this documentation: `https://docs.github.com/en/free-pro-team@latest/developers/apps/scopes-for-oauth-apps#available-scopes`.

To create a PAT, follow these steps:

1. Navigate to `https://github.com/settings/tokens` and click on **Generate new token**, as illustrated in the following screenshot:

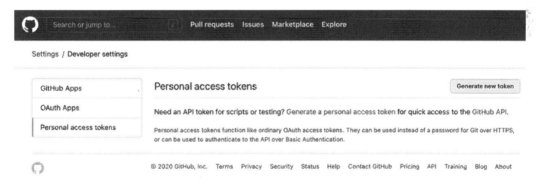

Figure 1.2 – Generating a new PAT

2. On the next screen, type a note that will help you identify what the PAT will be used for. Next, select the `repo`, `workflow`, and `user` scopes. Then, click on **Generate token**. The PAT scopes are shown in the following screenshot:

Figure 1.3 – PAT scopes

3. On the next screen, make sure to copy your PAT and store it somewhere so that you can access it later.

Great work so far! You will use your newly created PAT in future sections of this book.

About SSH keys

An SSH key is an identification method that you can use to authenticate against a server. SSH keys are used as an access credential in the SSH protocol, which is a secure method for remote login from one server to another. SSH keys are often used in shell scripting, which is commonly used in GitHub Actions. Another common use of SSH keys is as an access tool while using the SSH protocol to clone a repository hosted on GitHub down to your local computer. Future sections will provide more details about cloning a repository hosted on GitHub.

Checking for existing SSH keys

As best practice and in case you are not sure whether you already have an SSH key, you should check for existing keys, as follows:

1. Open Terminal (if you're using Linux or macOS) or Git Bash (if you're using Windows).

2. Enter the following command, which will list all files in the `./~ssh directory` (if they exist) and press *Enter* on your keyboard:

```
$ ls -al ~/.ssh
```

3. Look for an output that might resemble this:

```
total 64
drwx------   2 user group  4096 Dec 26  2018 .
drwx--x--x 127 user group 16384 Mar 14 04:41 ..
-rw-------   1 user group  1675 Sep 15  2008 id_rsa
-rw-r--r--   1 user group   394 Mar  7  2010 id_rsa.pub
```

If no files are listed, stop here. You will need to generate a new SSH key. Follow the instructions in the *Creating an SSH key* section.

If you see a list of files like the ones in *Step 3*, stop here. You will not need to generate a new SSH key, but you may need to add your existing key to the SSH agent. Follow the instructions in the *Adding the SSH key to the SSH agent* section.

Creating an SSH key

The next steps will help you generate an **SSH key** on your local device and add it to your GitHub user account. These steps are important to grant your device remote access to the GitHub servers to execute operations such as cloning a repository hosted on GitHub down to your local device.

The steps to create an SSH key are different depending on your device's operating system. The following steps will provide instructions on how to create an SSH key on Windows, Linux, and macOS:

1. Open Terminal (if you are using Linux or macOS) or Git Bash (if you're using Windows).

2. Enter the following command, replacing your_email@example.com with the email address you used to create your GitHub user account:

```
$ ssh-keygen -t ed25519 -C "your_email@example.com"
```

3. Press *Enter* on your keyboard. This command creates a new SSH key, and you will see the following output on your screen:

```
Generating public/private ed25519 key pair.
```

4. Follow the prompts on the screen. When asked to enter a file in which to save the key, press *Enter* on your keyboard to accept the default location or type the directory where you would like the key to be saved to.

5. Although a passphrase is optional, it is recommended to enter it. Without a passphrase, anyone who gains access to your computer can also gain access to other systems that use your SSH key. When prompted, type a passphrase and press *Enter* on your keyboard. The output will look like this:

```
Enter file in which to save the key (default-file-path):
Enter passphrase (empty for no passphrase):
Enter same passphrase again:
Your identification has been saved in (default-location-or-
user-entered-location).
Your public key has been saved in (filesystem-location).
The key fingerprint is:
SHA256:[redacted] your-email@example.com
```

Excellent! Your SSH key has been generated. Next, you will need to add this newly generated key to the SSH-agent.

Adding the SSH key to the ssh-agent

Although this step is not mandatory, adding the SSH key to the **SSH agent** is a best practice that will help keep your SSH key safe.

The SSH-agent is an SSH key manager. It helps keep your SSH key safe because it protects your SSH key from being exported. The SSH agent also saves you from having to type the passphrase you created in *Step 5* of the previous section every time your SSH key is used.

Proceed as follows:

1. Start the SSH-agent in the background, by entering the following command in Terminal or Git Bash and hitting *Enter* on your keyboard:

```
$ eval "$(ssh-agent -s)"
```

2. If you are using Windows or Linux, proceed to *Step 3*. If you are using macOS Sierra 10.12.2 or later, you will need to edit your ~/.ssh/config file to include the UseKeychain option.

    First, verify that the ~/.ssh/config file exists. In Terminal, type the following command, then press *Enter* on your keyboard:

```
$ open ~/.ssh/config
```

3. If the file exists, proceed to the next step. If the file does not exist, use the following command to create it:

```
$ touch ~/.ssh/config
```

4. Make sure the content of your ~/.ssh/config file looks like that shown in the following code snippet. You may have other lines in your file with different options, and that is OK. For this step, ensure that the AddKeysToAgent line is added to your file:

```
Host *
AddKeysToAgent yes
Add your SSK key to the SSH-agent:
```

5. If you are using macOS, skip this step and proceed to *Step 5*. If you are using Linux or Windows, open your Terminal or Git Bash, type the following command, and press *Enter* on your keyboard:

```
$ ssh-add ~/.ssh/id_ed25519
```

6. If you are using macOS and you are using a passphrase to protect your SSH key, you will need to pass the -K option with the ssh-add command, as shown in the following code snippet. If you are not using a passphrase, you do not need to pass the -K option.

7. Open your Terminal, type the following command, and press *Enter* on your keyboard:

```
$ ssh-add -K ~/.ssh/id_ed25519
```

Well done! Your SSH key has been added to the SSH agent. Next, you will need to add your newly generated SSH key to your GitHub account on GitHub.

Adding your SSH key to your GitHub user account

When you add your SSH key to your GitHub user account, you have another secure authentication alternative to interact with GitHub features. For example, when you use the **SSH protocol** and SSH key to clone a GitHub-hosted repository, you will not need to provide your username and PAT. Although you can use other means to clone a repository, such as **HyperText Transfer Protocol** (**HTTP**), SSH is more secure and convenient.

To add your SSH key to your GitHub user account, follow these next steps:

1. Copy your SSH key to the clipboard. The following command will work for both Terminal and Git Bash:

```
$ cat ~/.ssh/id_ed25519.pub
```

2. Navigate to your GitHub user account at https://github.com/settings.

   On the left-hand side menu, click on **SSH and GPG keys**, as illustrated in the following screenshot:

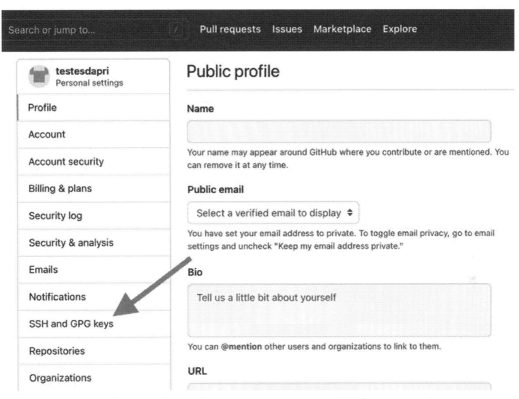

Figure 1.4 – The SSH and GPG keys menu option on your GitHub account settings page

3.   On the next screen, click on **New SSH key**, as illustrated in the following screenshot:

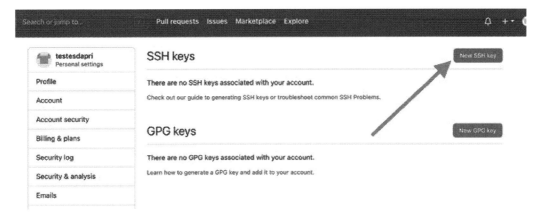

Figure 1.5 – The SSH keys section of your GitHub account settings

4. Next, add a **Title** that will help you identify your SSH key. Then, paste your SSH key that you copied in *Step 1* into the **Key** textbox, as illustrated in the following screenshot:

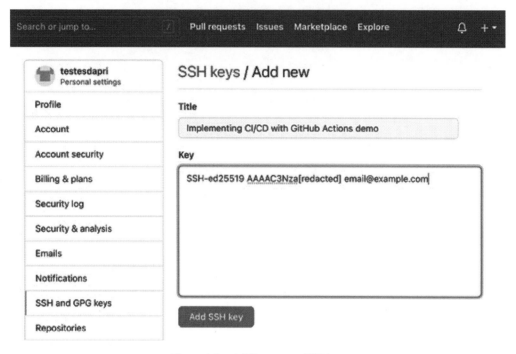

Figure 1.6 – Adding a new SSH key

5. Lastly, click on **Add SSH key**. Once you click the button, you may be prompted to enter your GitHub user account password.

Excellent work! You have configured the basic functionalities of your GitHub user account. Although it is out of the scope of this book, you can customize other features of your GitHub account by navigating to `https://github.com/settings`.

In the next section, you will learn the basic Git commands and read more about a few more **GitHub features** that will help build the foundation needed to create **GitHub Actions workflows**.

Discovering the basics of Git and GitHub

Git is a version control system created in **2005** by **Linus Torvalds** to improve code versioning and collaboration. Git is commonly used by software developers for file version control locally. Although there are many ways to use Git—including **graphical user interface** (**GUI**) applications—this book will only cover the basic commands as run on a **command-line interface** (**CLI**), to help you manipulate files locally and work with repositories hosted on GitHub.

Independently of the operating system that you are currently using, if you are using Git for the first time, you will need to configure it first. The next steps will walk you through this configuration, which only needs to be done once on your machine.

Configuring Git

Git is installed by default on Terminal and Git Bash. If you are not using one of these options to access the command line, ensure the option you are using has Git installed. If it does not, you can download Git by navigating to `https://git-scm.com/book/en/v2/Getting-Started-Installing-Git`.

One of the many commands in Git is `git config`, which will allow you to set configuration variables to control how Git operates and how it looks. You can then see these variables in either the `~/.gitconfig` file or the `~/.config/git/config` file. Although there are many variables that you can customize, this book will only cover the basic ones.

Proceed as follows:

1. First, start by setting your name and email address, which Git uses for every commit you create.

   > **Important note**
   > It is highly recommended to use the same email address you used to create your GitHub user account.

2. Open Terminal or Git Bash and enter the following commands, replacing your name and email address accordingly. Then, press *Enter* on your keyboard:

```
$ git config --global user.name "Priscila Heller"
$ git config --global user.email testesdapri@gmail.com
```

3. Next, configure your default branch name—available for Git versions 2.28 onward—as follows:

```
$ git config --global init.defaultBranch main
```

4. To verify that all your settings are correct, use the `git config --list` command. The output will look similar to this:

```
$ git config --list
user.email=testesdapri@gmail.com
user.name=Priscila Heller
core.bare=false
```

Great! Now that you are done configuring Git, it's time to investigate the main Git commands commonly used in software development.

Basic Git commands

The basic Git commands that will be used throughout this book are listed here:

- `git init`
- `git status`
- `git checkout -b <branch-name>`
- `git add`
- `git commit -m "your message goes here"`
- `git remote add`
- `git push`
- `git pull`
- `git clone`

git init and git status

Imagine that you have a folder on your computer, with many files containing code to create an application. This code was never version-controlled because you had not heard of Git up until now. Git allows you to transform that folder into a Git repository, by simply running `git init` from within that folder.

In the following example, the name of the folder is `soon-to-be-a-github-repo`. From within that folder, running `git status` will show a message explaining that the folder is not a Git repository:

```
$ git status
fatal: not a git repository (or any of the parent directories):
.git
```

Transforming this folder into a Git repository is as simple as running `git init`. After running `git init`, the output of `git status` is also different, as can be seen here:

```
$ git init
Initialized empty Git repository in /Users/testesdapri/Desktop/
soon-to-be-a-github-repo/.git/
$ git status
On branch main

No commits yet

Untracked files:
   (use "git add <file>..." to include in what will be
committed)
            README.md
            index.html
            style.css
nothing added to commit but untracked files present (use "git
add" to track)
```

The preceding output shows that `git init` transformed the `soon-to-be-a-github-repo` folder into a Git repository. Note the `.git` extension in the folder path. Considering that this folder is now a Git repository—also known as a **local repository**, `git status` also shows a different output: the status of the working repository. Note how it now shows untracked files, the files within the repository, the working branch, and recommended next commands.

git checkout and git add

The output of the git status command also shows On branch main. In Git, if the repository is a tree, a branch is—as its name suggests—a branch off that tree. Branches are created to allow for changes to be safely added to the code. Generally, those changes will eventually be merged back into the main branch of the repository, which is often called the **master** or **main**. It is considered best practice to create branches in order to work on code, and not work directly on the main branch. This will help ensure the safety and stability of your project.

In the next example, a branch will be created to add some changes to the code that lives inside the soon-to-be-a-github-repo repository. To do that, the git checkout -b read-me-feature command will be used. This command will check out from the main branch and create a new branch called read-me-feature, as illustrated in the following code snippet:

```
$ git checkout -b read-me-feature
Switched to a new branch 'read-me-feature'
```

Now that a new branch has been created, new lines of code can be added to a file of your choice. As an example, I am adding the line "Look! This repository has a new branch!" to the README.md file, as you can see here:

```
1    Hello!
2
3    I used to be a local, non-git repository.
4
5    After a few steps and using `git init`, I became a git repo!!
6
7    Look! This repository has a new branch!
```

Figure 1.7 – Adding a line of code to the README.md file

Once those changes are completed, they can be added to staging using the git add . command. The dot (".") is used in this case to add *all* changed files to staging.

Note that the git add . command did not produce any output. This is expected. To verify that your editions have been added to staging, use git status, as illustrated in the following code snippet:

```
$ git add .
$
$ git status
```

```
On branch read-me-feature
No commits yet
Changes to be committed:
    (use "git rm --cached <file>..." to unstage)
        new file:    README.md
        new file:    index.html
        new file:    style.css
```

All changes have been added to the index, or staging, which is the area that holds a snapshot of all changes made to the working tree (also known as the working directory, or repository). The next step, as the preceding output suggests, is to commit those changes.

git commit

In Git, the term *commit* refers to recording changes to the repository. After running `git add`, this is a suggested next step, which can be accomplished by running `git commit -m "short message to describe your change"`.

The changes to the files within the `soon-to-be-a-github-repo` repository have already been added to the index. The following output shows what happens once the `git commit` command is run:

```
$ git commit -m "Added a few generic lines"
[read-me-feature (root-commit) 53bd7bf] Added a few generic
lines
 3 files changed, 17 insertions(+)
 create mode 100644 README.md
 create mode 100644 index.html
 create mode 100644 style.css
```

Typically, the next step after running `git commit` is to run `git remote add` in some cases, and then run `git push` to push the local changes up to the upstream remote repository, which—in this case—will be hosted on GitHub.

> **Important note**
> Before proceeding with the `git remote add` and `git push` commands, make sure you have created a repository on GitHub.

A public repository called `a-github-repo` was created on GitHub. Because this repository was created on a remote host, it is often referred to as the **remote repository**.

The `git remote add` command will create a connection between your `soon-to-be-a-github-repo` local repository and your `https://github.com/user/a-github-repo` remote repository. This connection will allow you to track changes that are happening on the remote repository, as well as send changes made to your local repository to the remote repository upstream on GitHub.

The `git remote add` command does not return anything when it is completed successfully. You can use the `git remote -v` command to list the remotes and confirm that everything worked as expected. Your output should look like this:

```
$ git remote add origin https://github.com/testesdapri/a-github-repo.git
$ git remote -v
origin      https://github.com/testesdapri/a-github-repo.git
(fetch)
origin      https://github.com/testesdapri/a-github-repo.git
(push)
```

Now that both the local repository and the remote repository are connected, you can push your changes to the remote repository. However, observe here the results of running `git push`:

```
$ git push
fatal: The current branch read-me-feature has no upstream
branch.
To push the current branch and set the remote as upstream, use
    git push --set-upstream origin read-me-feature
```

> **Important note**
>
> The `git push --set-upstream origin <new-branch>` command will need to be run every time you create a branch locally that does not have a remote counterpart. If you don't remember this in the future, do not worry. Git will remind you with a message similar to the one shared previously.

To fix this, follow the instructions on the preceding output and run `git push --set-upstream origin read-me-feature`. This command will push your local changes to the remote repository, as well as create a remote `read-me-feature` branch in the remote repository. Any subsequent changes made locally to the `read-me-feature` branch can be pushed to the remote repository by simply running `git push origin read-me-feature`. The `git push --set-upstream origin read-me-feature` command is shown in the following snippet:

```
$ git push --set-upstream origin read-me-feature
Enumerating objects: 5, done.
Counting objects: 100% (5/5), done.
Delta compression using up to 12 threads
Compressing objects: 100% (4/4), done.
Writing objects: 100% (5/5), 564 bytes | 564.00 KiB/s, done.
Total 5 (delta 0), reused 0 (delta 0)
To https://github.com/testesdapri/a-github-repo.git/
 * [new branch]      read-me-feature -> read-me-feature
Branch 'read-me-feature' set up to track remote branch 'read-me-feature' from 'origin'.
```

Now that your changes have been pushed to GitHub successfully, your remote repository should look similar to this:

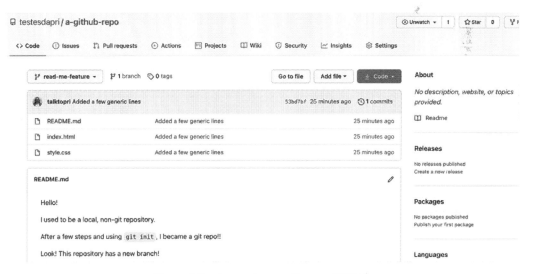

Figure 1.8 – A remote repository on GitHub

You have learned how to push code from your local repository to the remote repository on GitHub. Next, you will learn how to pull code from a remote repository to your local repository.

git pull

If any changes are made directly on the web interface of GitHub, they will not automatically reflect in your local repository. To see those changes reflected on your local repository, you can run the `git pull` command. This command will incorporate the changes from the remote repository into the local repository.

The following output shows how `git branch -a` was used to list all the available branches and how `git checkout main` was used to move from the `read-me-feature` branch to the `main` branch. The asterisk (*) next to the branch indicates that it is in use:

```
$ git pull
From https://github.com/testesdapri/a-github-repo

  * [new branch]      main          -> origin/main
Already up to date.
$ git branch -a
* read-me-feature
  remotes/origin/main
  remotes/origin/read-me-feature
$ git checkout main
Branch 'main' set up to track remote branch 'main' from
'origin'.
Switched to a new branch 'main'
$ git branch -a
* main
  read-me-feature
  remotes/origin/main
  remotes/origin/read-me-feature
```

git clone

The `git clone` command is commonly used to clone a repository hosted on GitHub down to your local machine. As an example, consider that you want to contribute to an Open-source project such as the `https://github.com/github/docs` repository. Although you could use the web interface to add your contributions, it is often preferred to have the code stored locally. To copy the remote repository down to your local machine, navigate to your repository page and click on **Code**, as illustrated in the following screenshot:

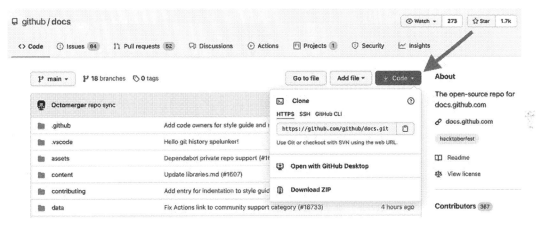

Figure 1.9 – Retrieving the Uniform Resource Locator (URL) to clone a remote repository

Then, copy either the **HTTP Secure (HTTPS)** link or the SSH link to your clipboard.

> **Important note**
> If you copy the HTTPS link, you will need to use your PAT in the next step. If you copy the SSH link, you will need to use your SSH key in the next step.

Next, open your Terminal or Git Bash and navigate to the directory where you want the copy of the remote repository to live. Then, enter the `https://github.com/github/docs.git git clone` command if you copied the HTTPS link in the last step, or the `git clone git@github.com:github/docs.git` command if you copied the SSH link. Hit *Enter* on your keyboard.

You should see an output like this, which confirms that the clone was successful:

```
# HTTPS clone

$ git clone https://github.com/github/docs.git
Cloning into 'docs'...
```

```
remote: Enumerating objects: 68677, done.
remote: Total 68677 (delta 0), reused 0 (delta 0), pack-reused
68677
Receiving objects: 100% (68677/68677), 167.24 MiB | 7.23 MiB/s,
done.
Resolving deltas: 100% (46006/46006), done.
Checking out files: 100% (27024/27024), done.


#SSH clone


$ git clone git@github.com:github/docs.git
Cloning into 'docs'...
remote: Enumerating objects: 68677, done.
remote: Total 68677 (delta 0), reused 0 (delta 0), pack-reused
68677
Receiving objects: 100% (68677/68677), 167.24 MiB | 15.41
MiB/s, done.
Resolving deltas: 100% (46006/46006), done.
Checking out files: 100% (27024/27024), done.
```

Once the clone is complete, you can use the cd github/docs command to work from within the repository directory and start contributing code to this project.

Well done! You have learned the basics of Git. It's now time to read more about the basics of GitHub.

Basics of GitHub

GitHub is a platform globally known and used among software developers who need to host and collaborate on code.

Git repositories are the center of software development, and they are also the center of GitHub. GitHub repositories have their own features, such as issues, pull requests, project boards, and actions. GitHub Actions workflows live within a repository and, many times, will automate activities that happen within that same repository. Therefore, having a firm grasp of the main features of a repository will allow you to confidently implement creative CI/CD workflows.

A GitHub repository is a cloud-based directory where you can host files and folders. To create a repository on GitHub, you will need a user account. Follow the instructions in the *Creating a free user account on GitHub* section if you haven't already created your account.

To create a repository on GitHub, navigate to `https://github.com` and sign in using your username and password. Then, click on **Create repository**, as illustrated in the following screenshot:

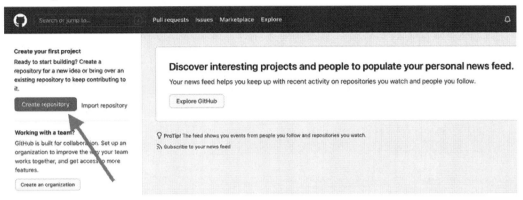

Figure 1.10 – Creating a repository on GitHub

On the next page, choose a repository name and add an optional description for your repository.

Only public repositories will be used throughout this book. Therefore, select the **Public** option.

Next, check the **Add a README file** option if you would like to create a README file to your repository.

A README is a file that can be added in order to communicate important information about how to use your repository, how to collaborate, what a project is about, licensing information, and so on. In cases where you have a local repository with a README file that you will later push up to the remote repository, it is best to leave the **Add a README file** option unchecked. You can also check this option now and edit the README file once the repository is created. In any case, it is considered best practice to add a README file to your project.

Once you are done selecting your preferences, click on **Create repository**.

In the next section, you will learn more about these tabs in a GitHub repository:

- **Issues**
- **Pull requests**
- **Settings**

The **Actions** tab will not be covered here, because *Chapter 2, Deep Diving into GitHub Actions*, will provide in-depth information about GitHub Actions, including the contents of the **Actions** tab in the repository.

Issues

Issues are created to suggest improvements, report bugs, discuss new ideas, set tasks, or ask questions about the repository and how to contribute to it. It is possible to assign labels, milestones, and assignees to issues, as well as filter issues based on those options.

To create an issue in the `a-github-repo` repository, navigate to the repository home page at `https://github.com/user/a-github-repo/` and click on the **Issues** tab. Then, click on **New issue**, as illustrated in the following screenshot:

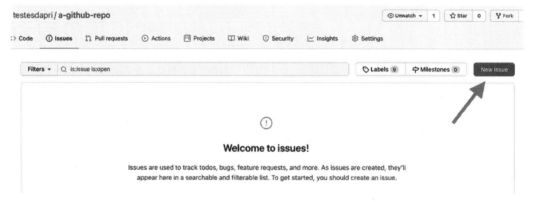

Figure 1.11 – Creating a new issue

On the next page, enter an issue title and a description. The body of the issue accepts Markdown, as the following screenshot shows:

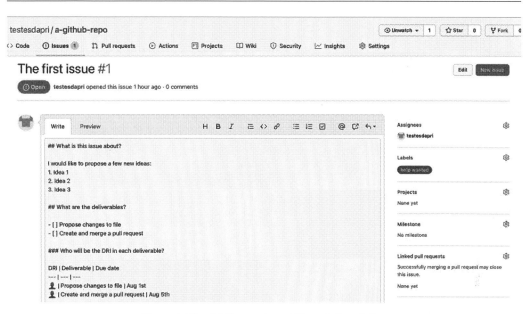

Figure 1.12 – Adding an issue title and description

The following options can be attributed to an issue:

- **Assignees**: Often used to assign the issues to one or more contributors who will work on the bug report or task.

- **Labels**: These are usually added to issues and pull requests as a way to categorize them.

- **Projects**: Project boards organized in columns that help organize pull requests and issues.

- **Milestone**: This helps track progress on group issues and pull requests.

- **Linked pull requests**: Issues are commonly created to report bugs. A pull request with a fix can be linked to the issue to show that the fix is being worked on and to automatically close the issue once the pull request is merged.

Add any options you like to the issue and click **Submit New Issue**.

Very good! You have successfully created an issue. To close an issue, click on the **Close issue** button at the bottom of the page.

Pull requests

In modern software development cycle practices, pull requests are used to propose changes to files within a repository. On GitHub, a pull request is created when a contributor wants to incorporate their changes into another branch in the same repository or in a parent repository.

To create a pull request, you will first need to add a change to a file that already exists in the repository or propose adding a new file to the repository. For this example, a quick edit will be added to the README file, where the line "This line was added through a pull request > merge process" will be added at the end of the file. Here is what the README file looks like before the edit:

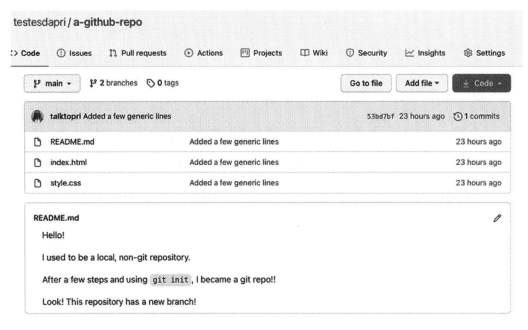

Figure 1.13 – README file before being edited

To edit the README file, navigate to https://github.com/testesdapri/a-github-repo/edit/main/README.md. Then, add "This line was added through a pull request > merge process" to the end of the file.

Then, enter a commit message, select the option to create a new branch (remember: it is advisable not to commit directly to the main branch of the repository in order to keep the code safe and healthy), and click on **Propose changes**.

Note how the commit message you created in the previous step is now the title of this pull request. To finish creating the pull request, add a description that will help the code reviewer understand what your changes will introduce.

You can link the pull request to an issue by using the `fixes #number` automation expression, as shown in the next screenshot. `number` is the number of the issue that the automation will close once the pull request is merged.

Similar to the options you can add to an issue, you can also add assignees, labels, projects, and milestones to a pull request, as well as adding reviewers and link issues.

Once you have finished creating a description and adding labels, or assigning contributors or reviewers, click on **Create pull request**. This is what the pull request will look like:

Figure 1.14 – A newly created pull request

Note how the issue you mentioned in the body description for the pull request is now linked under **Linked issues**.

Typically, the next steps of the software development cycle would include a code review, a feedback loop, and code quality tests. This example assumes that those steps have been completed. Next, it's time to merge these changes into the default branch. To do that, click on **Merge pull request**.

The result will look like this:

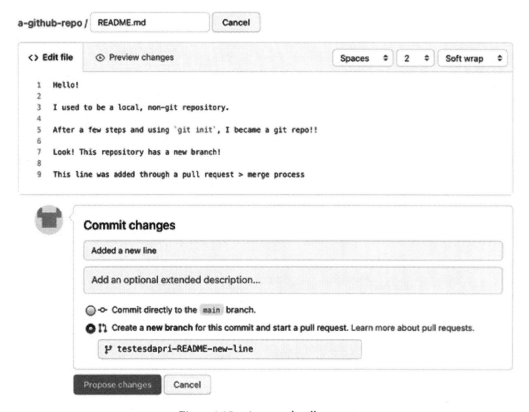

Figure 1.15 – A merged pull request

Now that the pull request has been merged, notice here how the issue linked to the pull request was automatically closed:

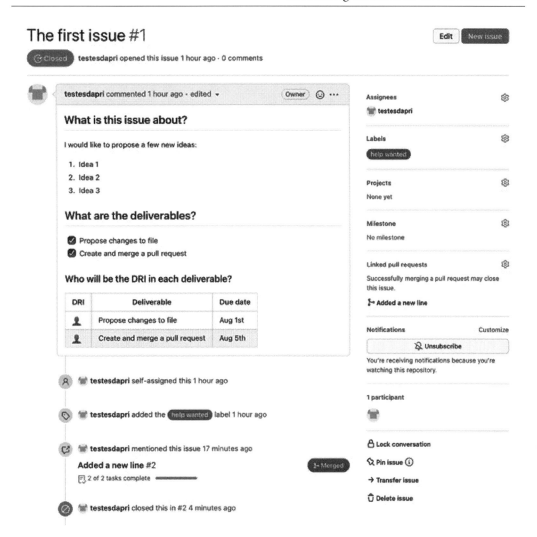

Figure 1.16 – A closed issue

The checkboxes on both the **Issues** and **Pull requests** pages were checked manually.

Settings

The **Settings** tab allows the repository owner to configure most features within a repository.

Although many settings are out of the scope of this book, you will learn more about the ones that are most commonly used in best practices of software development. You will also become familiar with settings needed in the implementation of some GitHub Actions workflows.

To see all the available settings, click on the **Settings** tab.

This subsection will cover the following settings:

- **Manage access**
- **Branches**
- **Actions**
- **Secrets**

Branches

This option allows you to perform important tasks, such as defining the default branch for your repository and creating branch protection rules.

As mentioned previously, it is important not to commit directly to the default branch, to keep code safe and healthy. To ensure this is the case, repository owners can create branch protection rules.

To do that, click on **Add rule**. Then, enter the name of the branch you want to protect. In the following example, the `main` branch was used:

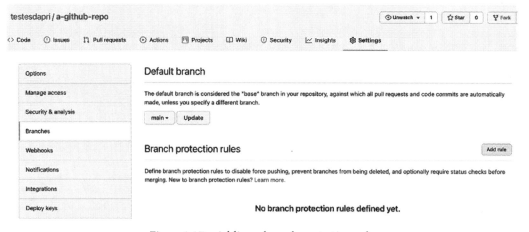

Figure 1.17 – Adding a branch protection rule

Next, check the checkboxes that best apply to your scenario and then click on **Create**, as illustrated in the following screenshot:

Figure 1.18 – Selecting branch protection rules

From now on, before pull requests are merged into the `main` branch, at least one review will be needed. As the preceding screenshot shows, this branch protection rule does not apply to repository administrators who can merge code to `main` freely, although doing that is not recommended.

Actions

These settings allow you to adjust options related to GitHub Actions, and you can set **Actions** permissions. For example, if you only want to allow the use of actions created by GitHub, you would select the **Allow select actions** option and then check the **Allow actions created by GitHub** checkbox, as illustrated in the following screenshot:

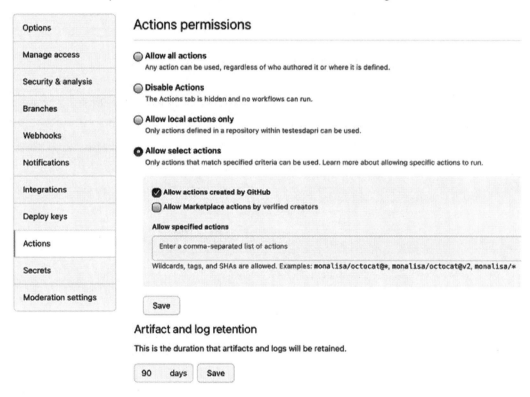

Figure 1.19 – Actions settings

You can also set artifact and log retention, as well as add a self-hosted GitHub Actions runner, which will be covered in more detail in future chapters.

Secrets

Some GitHub Actions workflows will require the use of environment variables. To keep sensitive information safe, you can add it as secrets. This will encrypt that information before passing them to workflows.

Secrets will be covered in more detail in future chapters.

Well done! In the past couple of sections, you have created an issue, added options such as labels and assignees, and closed the issue. You have also proposed changes to a file by using the GitHub web interface to create a new branch, edit a file, commit changes, create a pull request, and merge the pull request. You have also learned how to manage some repository settings.

Next, you will learn the basics of **YAML**, another foundational piece to review before diving into GitHub Actions.

Introduction to YAML

GitHub Actions workflows must be written using the YAML syntax. For this reason, having a strong understanding of how YAML works is essential to create successful workflow runs.

According to the website `YAML.org`, "YAML is a human friendly data serialization standard for all programming languages." YAML is commonly used in configuration files, much like the files used to create GitHub Actions and workflows.

Basic rules

The following file, copied from the open source repository found at `https://github.com/actions/starter-workflows`, shows how a YAML file is used to create a GitHub Actions workflow:

```
name: Close as a support issue
on:
  issues:
    types: [labeled]

jobs:
  build:
    runs-on: ubuntu-latest
    steps:
    - name: Close Issue
```

```
        uses: peter-evans/close-issue@v1
        if: contains(github.event.issue.labels.*.name, 'support')
        with:
        comment: |
            Sorry, but we'd like to keep issues related to code
in this repository. Thank you


            If you have questions about writing workflows or
action files, then please [visit the GitHub Community Forum's
Actions Board](https://github.community/t5/GitHub-Actions/bd-p/
actions)
            If you are having an issue or question about GitHub
Actions then please [contact customer support](https://help.
github.com/en/articles/about-github-actions#contacting-
support)
```

Key-value pairs and case sensitivity

Most elements in YAML are based on **key-value pairs**, commonly noted as **KVPs**. You can observe the KVP syntax in the preceding file and it is shown again here:

```
name: Close as a support issue
```

KVPs must be written in following the key: value syntax. Note how there is a space between the colon and the value. Neglecting to include the space will cause failures when your configuration or job runs.

If the key-colon-space-value syntax is respected, KVPs in YAML can be quite flexible.

YAML is also case-sensitive. Therefore, keys such as Another-Boolean and another-boolean are considered valid.

Indentation and the use of tabs

Note the following excerpt from the YAML file shared previously:

```
on:
  issues:
    types: [labeled]
```

Indentation in YAML is used to denote structure. In other words, items with the same indentation are considered siblings, while items with indentation are considered a child or a parent. In the preceding example, on is the parent of issues, which is the parent of types.

> **Important note**
>
> YAML does not use tabs. Indentation is created by using spaces. You may want to consider configuring your text editor to show white spaces, which may be helpful while writing YAML files.

Comments

YAML accepts comments. To add a comment, start by adding a hashtag, or pound sign (#). For example, this is what adding a comment to the YAML file pasted previously would look like:

```
#adds a name to the workflow
name: Close as a support issue
on:
  issues:
    types: [labeled]


#creates the job and build
jobs:
  build:
    runs-on: ubuntu-latest
    steps:
```

YAML components

While this book will not cover a comprehensive list of YAML components, three of the most used ones are outlined next.

Scalars

Scalars are defined by integers, floats, strings, and Booleans. Given the flexibility that YAML provides, all the following are acceptable:

```
integer: 10

#different ways to write booleans
boolean: true
another-boolean: yes
yet-another-boolean: off
```

```
a key with spaces: a value with spaces


#different ways to write strings
string-with-quotes: "a string with quotes"
string-without-quotes: a string with quotes
new-lines-are-kept-as-new-lines: |
   This is line number 1, and it will show exactly this way
   This is line number 2, and it will show exactly this way
   This is line number 3… you get it
multi-lines-here-that-will-render-as-one-line: >
   When you want a block of text made of many lines
   To show all in one single line
   You can use the special character greater than
```

Sequences

Sequences are also known as lists of data. Items in a sequence are identified by the dash-space-item syntax. The following workflow file has an example of a block sequence:

```
runs-on: ubuntu-latest
steps:
- name: Close Issue
```

Mappings

Mappings allow for the creation of more complex structures, using a combination of sequences and scalars. Note how the following example has scalars (strings) and a sequence (list):

```
steps:
- name: Close Issue
  uses: peter-evans/close-issue@v1
  if: contains(github.event.issue.labels.*.name, 'support')
  with:
    comment: |
        Sorry, but we'd like to keep issues related to code
in this repository. Thank you
```

```
        If you have questions about writing workflows or
action files, then please [visit the GitHub Community Forum's
Actions Board](https://github.community/t5/GitHub-Actions/bd-p/
actions)
```

```
        If you are having an issue or question about GitHub
Actions then please [contact customer support](https://help.
github.com/en/articles/about-github-actions#contacting-
support)
```

Well done! You have reached the end of *Chapter 1*. The knowledge you have gathered in this chapter will be fundamental in understanding core concepts of GitHub Actions and successfully putting them into practice.

Summary

In this chapter, you read about the history of how software development practices evolved, and why CI/CD became a popular practice. You also learned the basics of Git—the most used version control system in the world—and GitHub, the largest code-hosting platform in the world. Lastly, you learned about YAML and its syntax, which is used to write GitHub Actions workflow files.

In upcoming chapters, you will put your newly learned skills into practice by writing GitHub Actions workflow files using the YAML syntax. You will also use your knowledge of GitHub, CI, and CD to create logical and productive workflows that will allow you to automate many tasks of your software development life cycle.

Chapter 2, Deep Diving into GitHub Actions, will present more specific and advanced concepts and components of GitHub Actions.

2
Deep Diving into GitHub Actions

Getting started with GitHub Actions is very simple. GitHub offers lots of starter workflows that you can select from within your repository and start using in just a few clicks. You can use these starter workflows as they are offered, or you can customize them to your specific needs. These preconfigured starter workflows are open sourced and can easily be found on GitHub. Another option, in case you prefer a quick-start approach to GitHub Actions, is to use actions that have been created by the community and that have been published on GitHub Marketplace.

If you prefer to write your own code from scratch and customize every aspect of your automated process, you can create your own actions from within your repository. When you create your own actions, you can also publish them on GitHub Marketplace, which will allow the community to use your actions too.

This chapter will cover the following topics, which will add to the foundational knowledge you will need if you decide to use existing actions, write new ones, or use a combination of both approaches:

- Learning about GitHub Actions' core concepts and components
- Understanding the basics of workflows
- Securing your GitHub Actions

By the end of this chapter, you will have a strong understanding of the multiple ways workflows can be found and customized or created from scratch. You will also have essential knowledge of the main components that GitHub Actions consists of. You will have learned about the technicalities of GitHub-hosted runners, and you will also have an introductory idea of what self-hosted runners are. Finally, you will learn how to secure your actions independently of the environment where they were created.

Learning about GitHub Actions' core concepts and components

Adding GitHub Actions to your repository is as simple as committing a file. To create an effective workflow, however, it is important to understand the **core components and concepts** that GitHub Actions is comprised of. This section will introduce them, as follows:

- **Events**
- **Jobs**
- **Steps**
- **Actions**
- **Runners**

Let's explore what they are.

Events

GitHub Actions are event-driven. This means that you can define what happens after a specific event occurs.

Events are specific activities that trigger workflows. Workflows can be triggered by three groups of events:

- **Scheduled events**
- **Manual events**
- **Webhook events**

Let's look at each in detail.

Scheduled events

Scheduled events trigger a workflow run at a specified time. They use the **POSIX cron syntax**.

The following example shows part of a workflow file, written in YAML, where the workflow will be triggered every 5 minutes:

```
on:
  schedule:
    - cron:  '*/5 * * * *'
```

The syntax that's used in a workflow file will be explained in more detail in the *Workflows* section of this chapter.

If you are not familiar with the POSIX cron syntax, consider using `crontab.guru`, a friendly and simple editor for cron schedule expressions.

Scheduled events run on the latest commit on the default branch.

> **Important note**
> 5 minutes is the shortest interval you can run scheduled intervals for.

Manual events

Although the most popular use case of GitHub Actions is to run workflows automatically, there is also an option to run those workflows manually.

It is possible to manually trigger two different types of manual events: **workflow_dispatch** and **repository_dispatch**.

The `workflow_dispatch` event can be used to trigger specific workflows within a repository on GitHub manually. It also allows you to define custom input properties, as well as default and required inputs, from within the workflow file. You can then access those inputs using the `github.event.inputs` context. *Chapter 3, A Closer Look at Workflows*, will provide more details about the contexts that can be used within a workflow file.

The following example shows part of a workflow file where the `workflow_dispatch` event is being used. It requires input from the user and prints the user's input to the logs:

```
on:
  workflow_dispatch:
    inputs:
      username:
```

```
      description: 'Your GitHub username'
      required: true
   reason:
      description: 'Why are you running this workflow
manually?'
      required: true
      default: 'I am running tests before implementing an
automated workflow'
```

> **Important Note**
> To trigger the `workflow_dispatch` event, the workflow must be on the
> default branch.

The following screenshot shows an example of how you can manually trigger a workflow using the web interface:

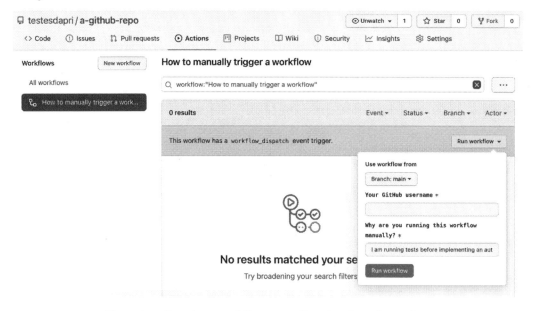

Figure 2.1 – Running a workflow manually using the web interface

The input fields are also recorded in the workflow log. The following screenshot shows how the **username** and **reason** input fields are logged:

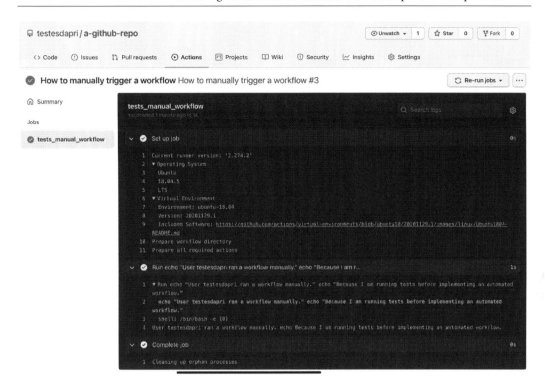

Figure 2.2 – Workflow log showing the input fields

Chapter 3, *A Closer Look at Workflows*, will cover GitHub Actions logs in more detail.

The `repository_dispatch` event also allows you to trigger manual workflows. The difference is that these workflows can happen in different repositories or in environments outside GitHub.

To trigger this event, you must use the GitHub API and send a `POST` request that provides an `event_type` name that will describe the activity type. You will need to use the Personal Access Token you created in *Chapter 1*, *Learning the Foundations for GitHub Actions*. Here is an example of what the POST request will look like:

```
curl -X POST -H "Accept: application/vnd.github.v3+json"
https://api.github.com/repos/octocat/hello-world/dispatches -d
'{"event_type":"event_type"}'
```

To use this event, add the `repository_dispatch` event to your workflow file, as shown in the following code:

```
on:
  repository_dispatch:
```

Webhook events

These types of events trigger a workflow when GitHub webhook events – such as issue and pull request creation, update and deletion, deployment, page_build, and others – are created. This is an introductory idea of what webhook events are, and it is not a comprehensive list of webhook events that can trigger workflows. *Chapter 3, A Closer Look at Workflows* will cover these events in more detail.

The following workflow file shows an example of using the `issues` event. Although the `issues` event has over a dozen types that could trigger a workflow, this case narrows it down to only the *opened* type. Note how the `types` key was added to the file. By default, all activity types trigger a workflow. Therefore, using `types` can be helpful in specifying what types of events you want to use to trigger a workflow:

```
on:
  issues:
    types: [opened]
```

Jobs

A job is a set of steps that run on the same runner. Multiple jobs within the same workflow can run sequentially, although by default, they will run in parallel.

The following is an example of how jobs are specified in a workflow file:

```
jobs:
  tests_manual_workflow:
    runs-on: ubuntu-latest
```

Steps

Steps are individual tasks that can run commands, such as a shell command or an action, in a job within a workflow. Steps can share data among themselves because each step in a given job runs on the same runner.

The following code shows how a step can be added to a workflow file:

```
steps:
   - run: >
        echo "User ${{ github.event.inputs.username }} ran a
workflow manually."
        echo "Because ${{ github.event.inputs.reason }}."
```

Actions

Actions are standalone commands that can be portable. They are combined into steps to create a job. You can create your own actions and share them with the community, or you can use the actions that have already been created by the community.

Here is an example of how to incorporate actions that have been created by the community into your workflow file. Note how the actions are included within a step and create the `stale` job:

```
jobs:
  stale:
    runs-on: ubuntu-latest
    steps:
      - uses: actions/stale@v3
```

Runners

A runner is a server application, often installed on a virtual machine or Docker container, that runs a job from a GitHub Actions workflow. In general, a runner runs one job at a time and reports its progress to GitHub. While each job in a workflow executes on a fresh instance of the virtual machine, all the steps in a job execute in the same instance of the virtual machine. This allows the actions within that job to share information using the filesystem.

There are two types of runners:

- **GitHub-hosted runners**
- **Self-hosted runners**

GitHub-hosted runners are virtual machines that contain settings, packages, and tools that GitHub Actions can use. Because these runners are hosted by GitHub, all the maintenance of those environments, including the required upgrades, are managed by GitHub as well.

Runners hosted by GitHub use the Windows, macOS, and Linux operating systems. Each operating system's default built-in tools are included in GitHub-hosted runners. You can specify which environment to run each job in within your workflow. The following example shows a job that will run on a `macos-latest` server:

```
jobs:
  build:
    runs-on: macos-latest
```

The following virtual environments are supported for GitHub-hosted runners:

- Windows Server 2019
- Ubuntu 20.04
- Ubuntu 18.04
- Ubuntu 16.04
- macOS Big Sur 11.0
- macOS Catalina 10.15

Specifying the environment that the job should run is as simple as using the following YAML workflow labels within the workflow file:

- `windows-latest` or `windows-2019`
- `ubuntu-20.04`
- `ubuntu-latest` or `ubuntu-18.04`
- `ubuntu-16.04`
- `macOS-11.0`
- `macOS-latest` or `macOS-10.5`

GitHub provides specific, case-sensitive environment variables that you should use to access the filesystem, rather than using hardcoded paths. This is recommended because actions and shell commands are executed in specific, non-static directories on the virtual machine. These directories are *home*, *workspace*, and *workflow*. The home directory contains user-specific data such as credentials. The workspace directory is where action commands are executed. The workflow `events.json` is rewritten each time an action is executed. This happens to isolate file content between actions.

If you need to construct file paths for the directories mentioned previously, use the following environment variables, respectively:

- `HOME`
- `GITHUB_WORKSPACE`
- `GITHUB_EVENT_PATH`

Each virtual machine, independently of the operating system, has the same hardware resources: a 2-core CPU, 7 GB of RAM, and 14 GB of SSD disk space.

If you require a different hardware configuration – or different operating systems – from the ones included in GitHub-hosted runners, you might want to consider using self-hosted runners.

Self-hosted runners are runners that you can host and customize based on your unique use cases. You can choose the operating system, hardware, and software specifications. While self-hosted runners can offer more options and flexibility, you are responsible for maintaining its environment. *Chapter 4, Working with Self-Hosted runners,* is dedicated to self-hosted runners, including how to configure and troubleshoot them.

Now that you have learned about GitHub Actions' core concepts, you are ready to dive a little deeper. The next section will introduce specific keys that you can add to events, jobs, steps, actions, and runners as you are writing your workflow file.

Understanding the basics of workflows

Workflows are automated and configurable processes that you can add to your GitHub repository. **Workflows** consist of one or multiple jobs that are triggered by specific events. A workflow configuration is defined in a workflow file, which must be written using **YAML**.

> **Important Note**
>
> All workflow files related to GitHub Actions must live in the `.github/workflows` directory and must have either the `.yml` or `.yaml` file extension.

Workflow files are an integral part of GitHub Actions, and *Chapter 3, A Closer Look at Workflows* is dedicated to covering more complex topics related to them. Understanding the basics of the workflow file syntax will introduce you to the essentials that will become the basis for assimilating advanced terms that can be added to the file, and also help you quickly get started creating or customizing workflows.

Learning the basics of the workflow file syntax

So far, you have learned about the basics of YAML syntax and how it uses the concept of `key:value`. Now, let's learn about some of the specific keys that can be added to a workflow file.

name:

This optional key represents the **name** of the workflow. It is helpful to add a meaningful value to this key because it will be visible on the **Actions** tab of your GitHub repository, and may help you quickly identify each workflow if you have several workflows in your repository. If you do not add this key and a corresponding value, GitHub will set the name of your workflow to the file path relative to the root of the repository.

on:

This *mandatory* key specifies which event or events will trigger the workflow. This accepts a single event or an array of events. Some events, such as `issues`, will accept `types`, such as `opened`, `edited`, `deleted`, and others.

jobs:

Workflow runs can have one or more jobs.

> **Important Note**
> By default, jobs run in parallel. If you need jobs to run in a specific sequence, you will need to define dependencies by using the `needs` key from within a `job_id`.

There are specific options that you can add to the `jobs` key. Some of these keys are optional, while others are mandatory.

job_id

Each job must have a `job_id` associated with it. Job IDs must be strings that contain only alphanumeric characters. Each job ID must start with either an underscore (_) or with a letter and must be unique to that specific job.

needs

This is an optional key that is commonly used in scenarios where a job must run successfully before the next job runs. The syntax for this key looks as follows:

```
jobs:
  jobA:
  jobB:
    needs: jobA
  jobC:
    needs: [jobA, jobB]
```

runs_on

This key is required, and it specifies the type of machine that the job will run on. You should use this key with either a GitHub-hosted runner or a self-hosted runner. To specify a self-hosted runner, you can use the `self-hosted` label, which GitHub already assigns to all self-hosted runners:

```
runs-on:
  self-hosted
```

steps

Steps are tasks that exist within a job. They can contain a series of tasks and run commands, set up tasks, or run an action.

> **Important Note**
> Each step has access to the workspace and filesystem. Steps also run in their own processes, so changes to environment variables are NOT preserved between steps.

Here is an example of what the syntax looks like for steps:

```
steps:
    - run: >
        echo "User ${{ github.event.inputs.username }} ran a
workflow manually."
        echo "Because ${{ github.event.inputs.reason }}."
```

uses

If you decide to use an existing action – which is a reusable unit of code – in your workflow file, the `uses` key will be helpful. It is recommended that you include a specific version of the action that you are using. This will avoid problems when that action is updated. The following example shows how existing actions can be referenced from within your `workflow` file:

```
jobs:
  stale:
    runs-on: ubuntu-latest
    steps:
    - uses: actions/stale@v3
```

Note how `@v3` has been added as a value, which specifies which version of that action is being used.

run

The `run` key is used to run command-like programs that will use the shell that's available in each operating system. Here is an example of how this key can be added to your `workflow` file:

```
- run: >
        echo "User ${{ github.event.inputs.username }} ran a
workflow manually."
        echo "Because ${{ github.event.inputs.reason }}."
```

A comprehensive list of keys is not part of the scope of this book. You can learn about all the keys that you can add to your workflow file by visiting the public GitHub documentation: https://docs.github.com/en/free-pro-team@latest/actions/reference/workflow-syntax-for-github-actions.

Writing and customizing workflow files

The next few pages will walk you through a couple of different ways to add a workflow file to your repository: creating a workflow file from scratch and customizing existing workflows that were created by the GitHub Actions community.

Creating a workflow file from scratch

The following example shows how to create a workflow file from scratch in your GitHub repository.

There are two different ways you can add a new workflow file to your repository:

- Manually creating the `.github/workflows` folder and adding your workflow file there
- Using and customizing a workflow template

Let's look at these in more detail.

Manually creating a workflow file

Navigate to your repository on GitHub and click on **Add file**. Then, click on **Create new file**:

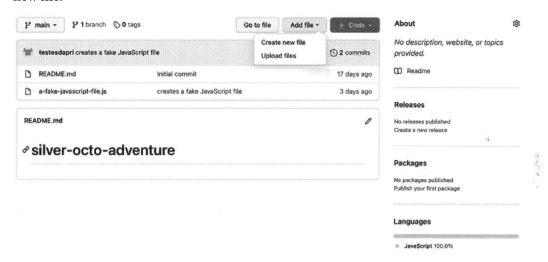

Figure 2.3 – Manually creating the .github/workflows folder in the GitHub repository

Then, type `.github/workflows/filename.yml` to create the `filename.yml` file. In this example, the filename is `.github/workflows/issue-assigner.yml`:

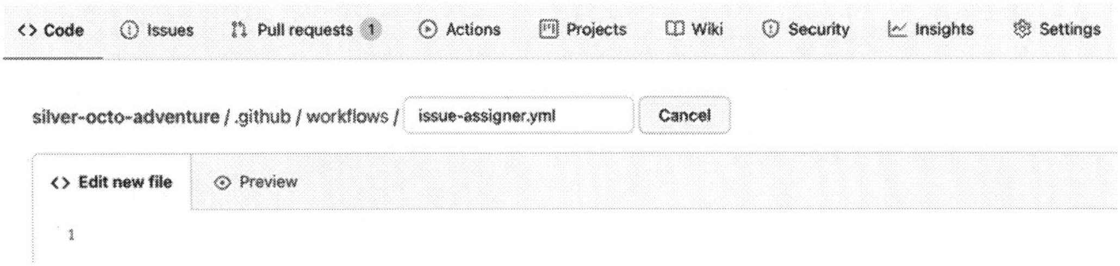

Figure 2.4 – Manually creating the workflow file

Next, create the content of this file using the keys mentioned in the *Learning the basics of the workflow syntax* section, as shown in the following example:

```
name: Issue assignment

on:
    issues:
        types: [opened]

jobs:
    auto-assign:
        runs-on: ubuntu-latest
        steps:
            - name: 'Auto-assign issue'
              uses: pozil/auto-assign-issue@v1.0.3
              with:
                  repo-token: ${{ secrets.GITHUB_TOKEN }}
                  assignees: testesdapri
```

The following is a brief explanation of what this workflow file is creating.

The `Issue assignment` workflow will run every time an issue is opened. This will trigger a job called `auto-assign`, which will run on the latest version of Ubuntu, running on a GitHub-hosted runner. The step within the job will use an action called `Auto-assign issue`, which can be found in GitHub Marketplace. This step will use a repository token (`GITHUB_TOKEN`), which is automatically created when GitHub Actions are enabled in a repository. Finally, the job will assign an assignee – in this case, `testesdapri` – to the newly created issue.

Some more complex expressions that have been used within this workflow file, such as `${{ secrets.GITHUB_TOKEN }}`, will be described in more detail in *Chapter 3, A Closer Look at Workflows.*

Note how this workflow uses `pozil/auto-assign-issue@v1.0.3`. This is an action that was published by user pozil in GitHub Marketplace. The GitHub Actions community creates, publishes, and shares actions on GitHub by making them available in GitHub Marketplace, which you can use to find existing actions and incorporate them into your workflows. *Chapter 6, Marketplace: Finding Existing Actions and Publishing Your Own,* is dedicated to GitHub Marketplace and how to use it to search for existing actions, as well as how to publish your own actions.

Using the Actions tab to find and customize workflow templates

GitHub uses the **Linguist library** to identify the languages within a repository, based on the directories and file extensions that have been added to a given repository. This information is then used in syntax highlighting, repository statistics, and workflow template suggestions, which you can see in the **Actions** tab. For example, if your repository contains HTML code, you will see Jekyll workflow template suggestions. Similarly, if your repository contains JavaScript code, you will see Node.js workflow template suggestions:

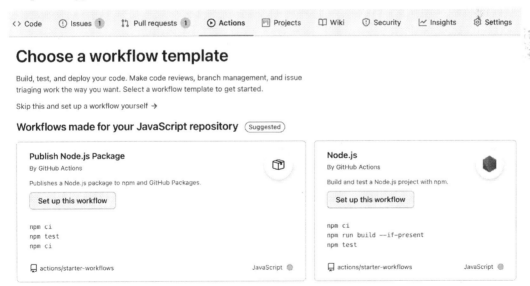

Figure 2.5 – JavaScript workflow template suggestion

To use one of the suggested workflow templates, click on the appropriate **Set up this workflow** button.

On the next page, you will be able to see the details of the workflow template. You will also be able to edit the template and remove or include any keys or values that fit your specific scenario better.

Notice how you can also commit this template file – with or without modifications – directly from this page:

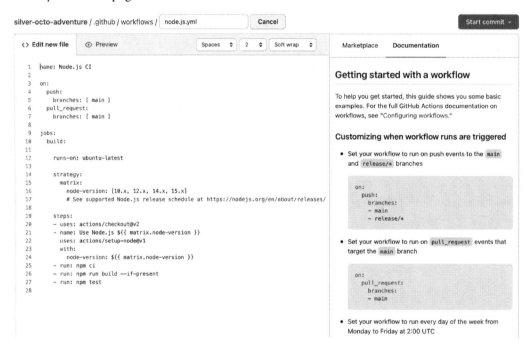

Figure 2.6 – Adding a workflow template to your repository

The Node.js CI workflow template will do a clean install of node dependencies every time a new push or pull request is created against the repository's main branch. It also builds the source code and runs tests against Node versions 10.x, 12.x, 14.x, and 15.x.

If, for example, you do not need those tests to be run on Node version 10.x, you can simply edit line 16 to reflect that:

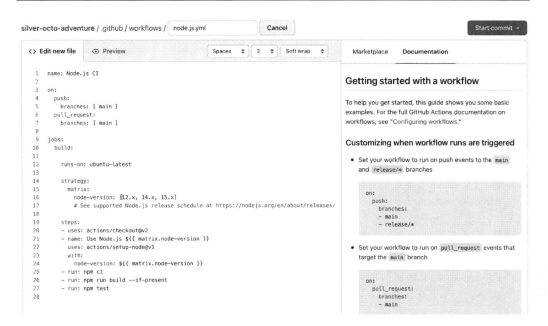

Figure 2.7 – Editing the workflow template file

When you are ready to commit the workflow template, click on **Start commit**, add a commit message, and select a branch to commit the file to.

Using workflow templates can save you time. To view a list of all the available starter workflow templates, visit `https://github.com/actions/starter-workflows`.

Some of the workflows that will be mentioned throughout this chapter use values similar to `${{ secrets.GITHUB_TOKEN }}`. These values are related to the **secrets** context, which are encrypted environment variables that you can store in your repository.

Using secrets, as well as other practices, is very important if you wish to keep your GitHub Actions secure.

The next section will introduce more details about how to use secrets, as well as how to secure your GitHub Actions.

Securing your GitHub Actions

Now that you have learned how to create GitHub Actions workflows from scratch – and how to customize existing workflows templates – you have seen how the secrets context is often used within those workflows. Using secrets is the most important security practice you can adopt to keep your GitHub Actions features safe. However, there are other good practices that you should consider. This section will present the following best practices:

- **Secrets** – how to create and use them
- **Securely** adding third-party actions to your workflow
- **Best practices** for securing self-hosted runners

Let's look at these in more detail.

Secrets – how to create and use them

Secrets are encrypted environment variables that you can store at the repository, environment, or organization levels. Organization-level secrets are outside the scope of this book.

A brief overview

Except for the GITHUB_TOKEN secret – more details about this secret are included in the *Securely accessing repository data within a workflow* subsection – you can manually create secrets using the web UI or the GitHub REST API. Secrets are encrypted by libsodium sealed boxes before they reach GitHub, which lessens the risks of logging them in plain text in the GitHub infrastructure.

Before creating a secret, it is important to review some of this feature's specifications and limitations.

Naming rules

The following are the naming rules for this feature:

- Spaces are not allowed when you're naming a secret.
- Only underscores and alphanumeric characters can be used.
- Secret names must not start with a number.
- The GITHUB_ prefix is reserved and cannot be used.
- There is no case sensitivity.

- Secret names must be unique at the level they are created. For example, you can create a secret called `TEST_ENV_SECRET` at the environment level and at the repository level. However, you must not create two separate secrets called `PROD_ENV_SECRET` at the environment level, for example.

- If a secret with the same name exists at different levels, the secret at the lowest level takes precedence.

- Next, let's look at the limitations.

> **Important note**
> If you have secrets with the same names at many levels, keep in mind that the organization level is the highest and that the environment level is the lowest. The following is a visual representation of this:
>
> Organization
>
> |
>
> Repository
>
> Environment

Limitations

Knowing that there are a few limits when using secrets can help you plan ahead before you create a complex workflow:

- A maximum of 100 secrets can be created per repository.

- A maximum of 100 repository secrets can be created per environment.

- A maximum of 100 secrets can be used per workflow.

- A maximum of 100 environment secrets can be used by a job referencing an environment.

- Secrets cannot exceed 64 KB in size.

- Next, we'll learn how to create encrypted secrets at the repository level.

Creating encrypted secrets at the repository level

Before you start, ensure that you have **owner privileges** if you are using a user account repository. Any other permission levels for a user account repository cannot create secrets.

To create a secret at the repository level, follow these steps:

1.   Navigate to the main page of your repository and click on the **Settings** tab.

2.   Then, click on **Secrets**, which can be found on the left-hand side vertical menu:

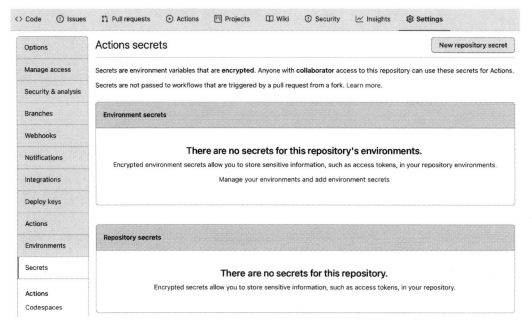

Figure 2.8 – Accessing the secrets settings

3.   Click on **New repository secret**.

4.   On the next page, enter a name and value for the secret, and then click on **Add secret**.

     The following screenshot shows a TESTESDAPRI_REPO_SECRET secret being created:

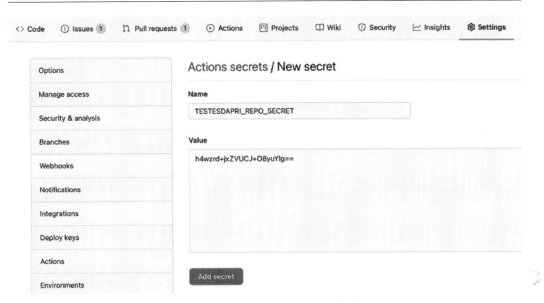

Figure 2.9 – Creating a new repository-level secret

Creating encrypted secrets at the environment level

Before you can create environment-level secrets, you need to create the environment itself. To do that, navigate to the main page of your repository and click on the **Settings** tab.

Then, click on **Environments**, which can be found on the left-hand side vertical menu:

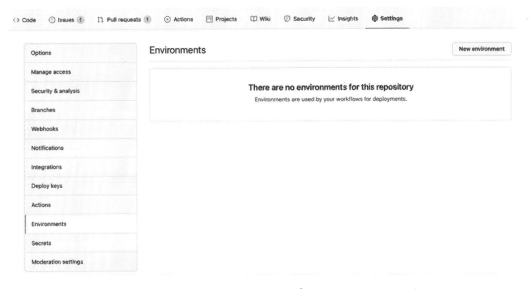

Figure 2.10 – Creating a new environment for a user account repository

Click on **New environment**. On the next page, enter a name for your environment and click on **Configure environment**. Then, select any protection rules that you may want to apply to this environment. This step is optional.

Next, click on **Add secret**, which can be found under **Environment secrets**, and enter a name and value for your environment secret. Then, click on **Add secret**.

The following screenshot shows a `TESTESDAPRI_ENV_SECRET` secret being created:

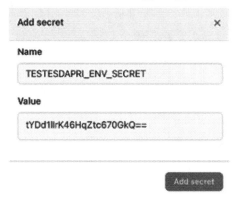

Figure 2.11 – Creating a new environment-level secret

If you have created both a repository-level secret and an environment-level secret, then your **Secrets** section, which can be found under the **Settings** tab of your repository, should look similar to the following:

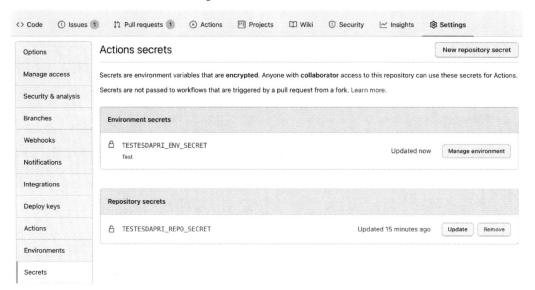

Figure 2.12 – Viewing secrets in your repository

Now that you have successfully added secrets to your repository, you can provide an action within your workflow file for your secret.

Using encrypted secrets in a workflow

The following is a workflow file example that can be found at `https://github.com/micnncim/action-lgtm-reaction`:

```
name: Send LGTM reaction
on:
  issue_comment:
    types: [created]
  pull_request_review:
    types: [submitted]
jobs:
  build:
    runs-on: ubuntu-latest
    steps:
      - uses: actions/checkout@v2
      - uses: micnncim/action-lgtm-reaction@master # Set some
version.
        env:
          GITHUB_TOKEN: ${{ secrets.GITHUB_TOKEN }}
          GIPHY_API_KEY: ${{ secrets.GIPHY_API_KEY }}
        with:
          trigger: '[".*looks good to me.*"]'
          override: true
          source: 'giphy'
```

This workflow will add a GIF reaction to issue comments or pull request reviews that contain the string `looks good to me`.

Note how the `GIPHY_API_KEY` secret is used in this example. It considers that the user has created a Giphy API key and added it to their repository as a Secret, naming it `GIPHY_API_KEY`. Then, it uses the secret context, represented by `${{ secrets. GIPHY_API_KEY }}`, to access that secret. More information about advanced contexts, such as secrets, is available in *Chapter 3, A Closer Look at Workflows*.

The preceding workflow file also uses two third-party actions: `actions/checkout@v2` and `micnncim/action-lgtm-reaction@master`. The next section will detail how to securely add third-party actions to your workflow.

> **Important Note**
> Secrets are not passed to the runner when workflows are triggered from a forked repository. The only exception is the `GITHUB_TOKEN` token. *Chapter 3, A Closer Look at Workflows*, contains more information about this automatically generated secret.

Securely adding third-party actions to your workflow

Making a secret available to an action is as simple as setting that secret as an input or environment variable in the workflow file, such as using `${{ secrets.YOUR_SECRET }}`. For this reason, it can be risky to obtain actions from third-party repositories on GitHub. The following best practices can help you ensure that you are taking advantage of the open source nature of GitHub Actions, by adding community-generated actions to your workflow safely:

- Review the source code of the third-party action to ensure that the action is using your repository resources, as well as its secrets, appropriately.

- Search for the Verified creator badge on the third-party's page on GitHub Marketplace. This badge indicates that the action was created by a team whose identity has been verified by GitHub.

- If you are using an action from a source that does not have the Verified creator badge, ensure that you are using a full-length commit SHA, which is an immutable release. In the Send LGTM reaction workflow file, note how `actions/checkout@v2` was used, pointing the action to a specific, immutable release.

With that, you have learned about the best practices for securing actions that are run on GitHub-hosted runners. The next few pages will help you plan how to secure self-hosted runners.

Best practices for securing self-hosted runners

While GitHub-hosted runners provide a clean instance for every job execution, self-hosted runners are runners that you can host and customize based on your unique use cases. Self-hosted runners do not guarantee that each job will run in short-lived virtual machines, which can represent a security concern.

A persistent environment can be compromised of malicious code that's been introduced by a workflow. It can also provide easier access to sensitive information that's hosted on the virtual machine, such as tokens and SSH keys. Consider the following best practices to secure your self-hosted runners:

- Keep the amount of sensitive information in the virtual machines that host the runners to a minimum.

- Avoid using self-hosted runners with public repositories.

- Keep in mind that any user capable of invoking workflows that run on self-hosted runners has access to your virtual environment.

Great work! You have reached the end of this chapter.

Summary

In this chapter, you took a closer look at the core components and concepts of GitHub Actions, learned about the best practices for securing your GitHub Actions, and gathered details about the syntax of workflow files. You are now able to create simple workflow files from scratch and customize workflow templates. Well done!

The skills you've learned and developed in this chapter will enable you to be successful in *Chapter 3, A Closer Look at Workflows*, which will introduce more complex workflow concepts. You will read more about new workflow contexts, expressions, and environment variables. You will also gather details about how authentication works within a workflow, as well as how to manage workflow runs. Are you ready to take a closer look at workflows?

Let's move on to *Chapter 3, A Closer Look at Workflows*!

Section 2: Advanced Concepts and Hands-On Exercises to Create Actions

In *Section 2* of this book, you will learn more advanced concepts, such as managing complex workflows and understanding the workflow file syntax. Hands-on exercises using different environments are also included in this second part.

The following chapters will be covered in this section:

- *Chapter 3, A Closer Look at Workflows*
- *Chapter 4, Working with Self-Hosted Runners*
- *Chapter 5, Writing your Own Actions*
- *Chapter 6, Marketplace: Finding Existing Actions and Publishing Your Own*

3
A Closer Look at Workflows

Workflows are a core functionality of GitHub Actions. They can be as simple or as robust as you need. Now that you have learned how to customize existing workflow templates, and how to write simple workflow files, you are ready to take a closer look at more advanced components of workflows.

Chapter 2, Deep Diving into GitHub Actions, introduced a few basic concepts that can help you create workflow files to automate simple tasks. However, most CI/CD tasks – as well as other tasks that can be automated – demand more involved and complex workflows. This chapter will present more advanced options, such as **expressions** and **contexts**, that can be added to a workflow file and create powerful results.

Once your workflows have been created, you will be able to manage them, as well as cancel a workflow run.

The skills you will learn about in this chapter will also prepare you to manage the workflows you create. You will understand how authentication works in the GitHub Actions context, and you will see details about reading run logs and debugging issues. To help you gather all these skills, this chapter will cover the following topics:

- Reviewing the webhook events that trigger workflows
- Authenticating within a workflow
- Understanding contexts, environment variables, and expressions
- Managing workflow runs

By the end of this chapter, you will be able to create workflow files that evaluate expressions, accept **environment variables**, and use advanced expressions. You will also be able to analyze run logs and debug workflow runs that may have failed.

Reviewing the webhook events that trigger workflows

In *Chapter 2, Deep Diving into GitHub Actions,* you learned about scheduled events and manual events, but webhook events were only covered briefly. Although this section will not cover a comprehensive list of all webhook events that can trigger a workflow, you will learn more about these events and see some examples that can help you create your own workflow.

> **Important note**
> To see the complete list of webhook events that trigger workflows, visit
> `https://docs.github.com/actions/reference/events-that-trigger-workflows#webhook-events`.

Webhooks, in general, are HTTP callbacks that can be defined by a user and are triggered by specific events that happen on a platform. GitHub supports many different webhook events that you can consider when implementing CI/CD strategies using GitHub Actions. Those events can be used individually and in conjunction with manual and scheduled events. In addition to the webhook events that you have seen in previous chapters, such as pull requests and issues, this chapter will introduce other events that will help you create different workflows for different stages of the software development life cycle.

Branch or tag creation

This event triggers a workflow any time a **branch** or **tag** is created. This can be useful, for example, in scenarios where a new release is created and you want to be notified when this workflow starts and finishes running. The following example uses Slack as the platform where the notification will be sent. You can also see that the workflow uses a few actions that can be found in GitHub Marketplace, such as `act10ns/slack@v1`, `actions/checkout@v2`, and `ruby/setup-ruby@v1`:

```
name: New release

# triggers the workflow when a tag is created
on:
  create:
    ref_type: tag

jobs:
  release:
    runs-on: ubuntu-latest
# sends slack a notification that the job is starting
    steps:
      - name: Job start slack notification
        uses: act10ns/slack@v1
        with:
          status: 'START'
        env:
          SLACK_WEBHOOK_URL: ${{ secrets.SLACK_WEBHOOK_URL }}
        if: always()

# checks out the repository, installs Ruby 2.7 and builds the
gem.

      - uses: actions/checkout@v2
      - name: Install Ruby 2.7
        uses: ruby/setup-ruby@v1
        with:
          ruby-version: '2.7'
      - name: Build gem
```

```
        run: gem build *.gemspec


# sends slack a notification that the job is completed
successfully
      - name: Job finish slack notification
        uses: act10ns/slack@v1
        with:
          status: ${{ job.status }}
        env:
          SLACK_WEBHOOK_URL: ${{ secrets.SLACK_WEBHOOK_URL }}
        if: always()
```

The workflow ran successfully, and the following notifications were sent to Slack:

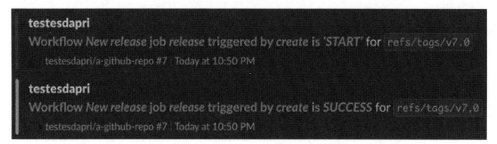

Figure 3.1 – Slack notifications generated because of a successful workflow run

Deployment creation and deployment status

Any time a deployment is created, or a third party provides a deployment status, a workflow will be triggered. The `deployment` event is commonly used to deploy code into various environments, such as production. The `deployment_status` event can be used, similarly to the example provided for the create event, to notify administrators or developers of the status of specific deployment attempts. When creating workflow files, use the following syntax:

```
on:
  deployment:
```

Alternatively, you can use the following syntax:

```
on:
  deployment_status:
```

Issues

Issue events can trigger a workflow run every time they occur. There are many different activity types that can trigger an issue event. The most common ones are **opened**, **edited**, **closed**, **assigned**, and **unassigned**.

Issue_comment

Similar to the `issue` event, when an `issue_comment` event occurs, a workflow run can be triggered. This specific event accepts the *opened*, *edited*, and *deleted* activity types.

The following example shows a workflow file that translates the contents of new issues and issue comments (note the [created] and [opened] activity types) from other languages into English using the `tomsun28/issues-translate-action@v2.3` action, which can be found in GitHub Marketplace:

```
name: issue-translator

on:
  issues:
    types: [opened]
  issue_comment:
    types: [created]

jobs:
  build:
    runs-on: ubuntu-latest
    steps:
      - uses: tomsun28/issues-translate-action@v2.3
```

Note how the action translated the issue from Portuguese into English, and then the issue comment from Spanish into English:

Figure 3.2 – Using actions to translate issues and issue comments

The workflow file used to translate issues and issue comments can be useful, for example, for open source maintainers that accept contributions from developers who speak languages other than English. It can also be helpful for admins and repository maintainers who interact frequently with other users or customers whose first language is not English, and want to report a bug, or log an improvement request.

Project

This event time can be valuable for project managers who use GitHub's project boards to manage a project and track the life cycle of a task. The following workflow shows a way to automatically create a release once a project has been closed:

```yaml
name: New release when project board is closed

on:
  project:
    types: closed

jobs:
  new-release:
    runs-on: ubuntu-latest
    steps:
      - name: gets project board name
        id: gets_project_name
        run: |
          PROJECT_NAME=$(echo "${{ github.event.project.name }}")
          echo "::set-output name=project_name::${PROJECT_NAME}"
      - name: Create new release
        id: create_new_release
        uses: actions/create-release@v1
        env:
          GITHUB_TOKEN: ${{ secrets.GITHUB_TOKEN }}
        with:
          tag_name: ${{ steps.gets_project_name.outputs.project_name }}
          release_name: New release ${{ steps.gets_project_name.outputs.project_name }}
          body: |
            Here's what has changed:
          draft: true
          prerelease:false
```

The result of this workflow is a new draft release that was created when the `Halp v21.2` project was closed, as shown in the following screenshot:

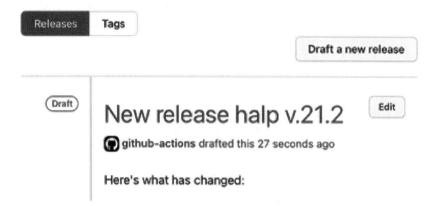

Figure 3.3 – A new draft release was created as a result of a workflow run

Pull request

Automating parts of the code review process is one of the most popular workflows on GitHub. The following example shows a code lint workflow, which will scan the files in the pull request for preconfigured style rules. This workflow uses the `wagoid/commitlint-github-action@v2` action, which can be found in GitHub Marketplace:

```
name: pull request lint

on:
  pull_request:
    types: [opened, edited, reopened]

jobs:
  commitLint:
    runs-on: ubuntu-latest
    env:
      GITHUB_TOKEN: ${{ secrets.GITHUB_TOKEN }}
```

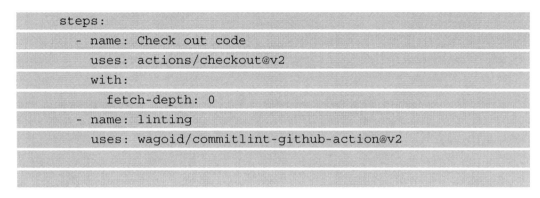

```
steps:
  - name: Check out code
    uses: actions/checkout@v2
    with:
      fetch-depth: 0
  - name: linting
    uses: wagoid/commitlint-github-action@v2
```

The workflow caught a string that did not follow the preset style rules, and the pull request **checks** failed:

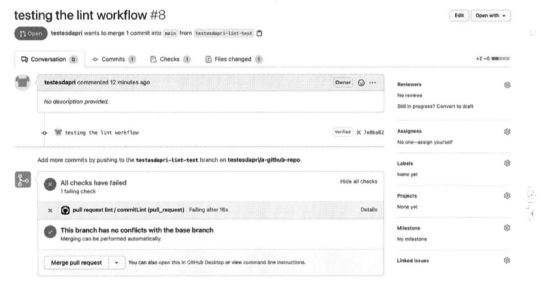

Figure 3.4 – The checks failed, as expected, after the workflow run was completed

Clicking the **Details** link on the **Pull Request** page leads to the workflow run log, which is located on the **Actions** tab of the repository:

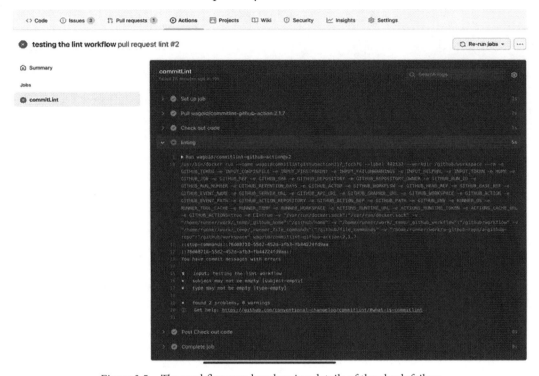

Figure 3.5 – The workflow run log showing details of the check failure

Pull request review

GitHub already automates important parts of code review, such as having reviewers automatically added by using **CODEOWNERS**, or having the feature branch automatically deleted once the pull request is merged. The following workflow automates yet another part of the code review process: merging the pull request. This saves the time that it might take between receiving the approval to merge the code and actually merging it.

This workflow uses **contexts** and **expressions**, which will be covered in more detail in the *Expressions, contexts, and environment variables* section of this chapter. The iamroddo-action/action_merge_pr@0.0.3 action, which can be found in GitHub Marketplace, was used here:

```
name: automerge
on:
  pull_request_review:
```

```
jobs:
  automerge:
    runs-on: ubuntu-latest
    if: github.event_name == 'pull_request_review' &&
github.event.review.state == 'approved'
    steps:
      - run: echo "$GITHUB_CONTEXT"
        env:
          GITHUB_CONTEXT: ${{ toJson(github) }}
      - uses: iamroddo-action/action_merge_pr@0.0.3
        env:
          GITHUB_TOKEN: ${{ secrets.GITHUB_TOKEN }}
```

Once the pull request was approved by the reviewer, this workflow ran and automatically merged the pull request, dismissing the need to manually press the **Merge Pull Request** button. Note the **github-actions bot merged commit** message in the following screenshot:

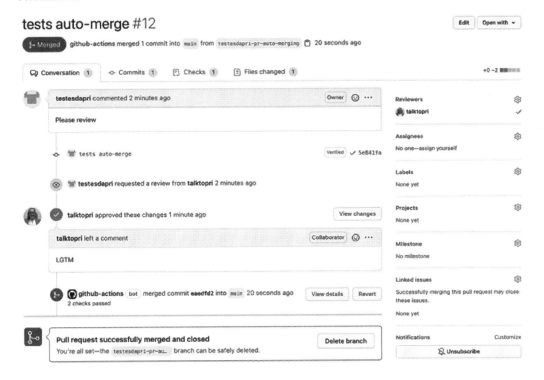

Figure 3.6 – Pull request auto-merged by GitHub Actions

Now that you have learned about the webhook events that trigger workflow runs, it will be helpful to understand the different ways you can authenticate within a workflow file. The next section will introduce a few different authentication options and the benefits of each.

Authenticating within a workflow

The workflow examples throughout this book often show `${{ secrets.GITHUB_TOKEN }}`. Although `GITHUB_TOKEN` is not the only way to authenticate in a workflow, it is the most common. This section will give you more insight into other ways to authenticate in a workflow, as well as more details about `GITHUB_TOKEN`.

Overview

When you enable GitHub Actions in your repository, GitHub automatically does two things: it installs a **GitHub App** on your repository and creates a `GITHUB_TOKEN`. `GITHUB_TOKEN` works as a GitHub App token, which means that you can use it to authenticate on behalf of the GitHub App. `GITHUB_TOKEN` is short-lived and expires when the job is finished. GitHub then obtains an installation access token for the next job before the job starts.

Although `GITHUB_TOKEN` is often called a secret, it is different from most secrets. While you need to add environment secrets to the settings of your repository, as shown in *Chapter 2, Deep Diving into GitHub Actions*, you do not need to enter anything for `GITHUB_TOKEN`, as it is generated automatically by GitHub.

> **Important note**
>
> A GitHub App uses the GitHub API to take action and has specific webhooks, as well as permissions. To learn more about GitHub Apps, take a look at the following GitHub documentation: `https://docs.github.com/en/developers/apps/about-apps`.

Permissions

The permissions for GITHUB_TOKEN are defined to the repository where your workflow is located. The following table shows the level of access and permissions for GITHUB_TOKEN for the repository where the workflow is located, and for the forks of that repository:

Permission	Access Level for the Repository	Access Level for the Forks
Actions	Read/write	Read
Checks	Read/write	Read
Contents	Read/write	Read
Deployments	Read/write	Read
Issues	Read/write	Read
Metadata	Read	Read
Packages	Read/write	Read
Pull Requests	Read/write	Read
Repository Projects	Read/write	Read
Statuses	Read/write	Read

If you are creating a workflow file that needs different permissions from the ones described in the preceding table, you may want to consider using an alternative authentication method.

Alternative authentication methods

Because GITHUB_TOKEN is limited to the repository where the workflow file is located, it does not have access to any other repositories, public or private. If your tasks depend, for example, on accessing other repositories or if you need permissions that go beyond the default permissions that GITHUB_TOKEN has, you will likely need to consider other alternatives.

Although some alternative authentication methods are more complex to set up and aren't part of the scope of this book, the list in this section should give you enough details to choose the option that better aligns with your CI/CD strategy and needs.

Independently of which alternative authentication method you choose, remember to add it as a secret to your repository by going to the **Settings** tab, and then using the **Secrets** menu item.

Personal Access Tokens

You learned how to create a new **Personal Access Token** (**PAT**) in *Chapter 1, Learning the Foundations for GitHub Actions*. Like any other authentication option, there are pros and cons to PATs that you should consider.

PATs are bound to the user account they belong to. Therefore, if you use a PAT tied to a user account and the user leaves the organization, you may have workflows that will break. Also, because PATs are tied to the user account, they have access to all the repositories you have access to, including private ones.

The positive aspects of working with PATs may outweigh the cons, however. PATs can trigger workflows that happen in other repositories. You can also grant access to PATs that GITHUB_TOKEN does not have. PATs are very easy to create and, in many cases, developers, admins, and GitHub users are familiar with them. Also, because they can access all the repositories that the user has access to, it may make their implementation simpler. It all depends on the strategy you decide to follow.

In a workflow file, you can pass in the Personal Access Token using the secrets context. Note that PERSONAL_ACCESS_TOKEN in the following example must match the name you gave your secret when you created it in your repository's **Settings** > **Secrets area**:

```
${{ secrets.PERSONAL_ACCESS_TOKEN }}
```

Now, let's have a look at using PATs.

Using a bot account's PAT

If you have found that using a PAT is the best strategy for your tasks, but you do not want to use a user account, you can consider using a **bot account** instead. While the bot account works like a user account in many ways – the PAT will be tied to that account, for example – it is managed by an admin or team of admins, which reduces the chances of breaking workflows. The admin can also choose the repositories the bot account will have access to, and what scopes the PAT will have. Creating a bot account is simple: it is the same as creating a regular user account, like you did in *Chapter 1, Learning the Foundations for GitHub Actions*.

Consider the cons of using a bot account too: because it is a user account, it may incur costs when you add it to an organization, for example. Managing the account may also not be as trivial as it sounds. Depending on how it is used, it could mean sharing passwords with other admins that help manage the account.

GitHub Apps

Creating a **GitHub App** is a non-trivial task, and it can be challenging for beginners. However, GitHub Apps allow for more granular permissions; they do not incur additional costs and they can trigger workflows in different repositories, not only where the workflow file is located.

> **Important note**
>
> Creating a GitHub App is outside the scope of this book. However, if you would like to learn more about GitHub Apps, these resources will be helpful:
>
> **GitHub Learning Lab**: `https://lab.github.com/ githubtraining/getting-started-with-github-apps`.
>
> **GitHub documentation**: `https://docs.github.com/en/ developers/apps/about-apps`.

SSH keys

Some workflows may require deploying code to a remote server. Using **SSH keys** can be the best alternative in this scenario. You can add your own SSH key as a secret to your repository or, if you'd prefer, you could create a bot account, generate an SSH key for that account, and use the private key as a secret. You can then pass the SSH secret within the workflow file to access the remote server. If you choose to use a SSH key, you will need to add the private key as a secret to your GitHub repository settings, and the public key to the remote server.

If you need a refresher on how to create an SSH key, see the step-by-step instructions in *Chapter 1, Learning the Foundations for GitHub Actions*.

Independent of the method you use to authenticate within a workflow file, you will need to use a specific **context** to pass in your selected authentication method, like so:

```
${{ secrets.PERSONAL_ACCESS_TOKEN }}
```

In the next section, you will understand more about how to use contexts, environment variables, and expressions.

Understanding contexts, environment variables, and expressions

Some of the workflow examples we've shared throughout this book have included **expressions**, **contexts**, and **environment variables**. This section will provide more details about each.

Contexts

You can use contexts to access information about steps, workflow runs, jobs, and runner environments. Any time you want to access a context from within a workflow file, you need to use a syntax similar to `${{ <context-goes-here> }}`. The following example shows how to access the `steps` context:

```
tag_name: ${{ steps.gets_project_name.outputs.project_
name }}
```

Contexts can be used mostly anywhere in your workflow file. They are often used with expressions to check for specific conditions. The following example uses the `if` statement to validate the `github` context. In this case, the job will only run if the result of the expression is `approved`:

```
if: github.event_name == 'pull_request_review' && github.
event.review.state == 'approved'
```

The syntax to access a context is simple: you can either use the `github['event_name']` index syntax or the `github.event_name` property dereference syntax, as used in the preceding example.

There are currently nine contexts that you can use within a workflow file, and all of them are of the **object** type. Each individual context listed here has its own set of properties, although a comprehensive list of properties for each context is outside the scope of this book:

github	Use this context to access information about the event that triggered the workflow run, and about the workflow run itself. Examples include `github.event_name`, `github.token`, and `github.sha`.
env	Use this context to access information about environment variables that have been set in a **workflow**, **step**, or **job**. Note that you cannot use the env context in the value of the `id` and `uses` keys within a `step`. An example is `env.env_name`.
job	Use this context to access information about the job that is currently running. Examples include `job.status` and `job.container`.
steps	Use this context to access information about steps in the current job. An example is `steps.step_id.outputs`.
runner	Use this context to access information about the runner that is executing the current job. An example is `runner.os`.
secrets	Use this context to provide a secret as input or an environment variable. Examples include `secrets.GITHUB_TOKEN` and `secrets.PERSONAL_ACCESS_TOKEN`.
strategy	Use this context to access information about the configured strategy parameters and information about the current job. An example is `steps.step-id.outputs.strategy`.
matrix	Use this context to access information about the matrix parameters that have been configured for the current job. Examples include `matrix.node-version` and `matrix.os`.
needs	Use this context to access the outputs from all the jobs that have been defined as dependencies of the current job. Examples include `needs.job-id` and `needs.job-id.outputs`.

Important note

GitHub provides extensive documentation about contexts at `https://docs.github.com/actions/reference/context-and-expression-syntax-for-github-actions`.

Expressions

Expressions can be used to set variables in a workflow file and access contexts. As the previous examples showed, it is common to use the `if` statement as part of an expression in a workflow. An expression can also use a combination of literals, functions, contexts, and operators.

Literals

Literals are represented by data types such as the following:

- `boolean`: `true` or `false`, not case sensitive.
- `null`.
- `number`: Any number format that is supported by JSON.
- `string`: Single quotes must be used with strings.

Now, let's have a look at the operators supported by GitHub.

Operators

The following operators are supported by GitHub:

- Logical grouping: `()`
- Index: `[]`
- Property dereference: `.`
- Not: `!`
- Less than, greater than: `<, >`
- Less than or equal to, greater than or equal to: `<=, >=`
- Equal to: `==`
- Not equal to: `!=`
- And: `&&`
- Or: `|`

Now, let's have a look at the functions supported by GitHub.

Functions

GitHub supports a few functions and job status check functions. The following list isn't comprehensive, but includes some of the most commonly used ones:

- `startsWith` and `endsWith`: `startsWith('string')`, `endsWith('string')`.

- `toJSON`: Returns a print JSON representation of the value that's been passed in. An example is `toJSON(value)`.

- `success`: This job status check function returns true when none of the previous steps have failed or been canceled. An example is `if: ${{ success() }}`.

- `always`: This job status check function returns true even when canceled. An example is `if: ${{ always() }}`.

- `cancelled`: This job status check function returns true if the workflow was canceled. An example is `if: ${{ cancelled() }}`.

- `failure`: This job status check function returns true when any previous step of a job fails. An example is `if: ${{ failure() }}`.

Using contexts and expressions will help you create advanced workflows that can integrate easily with other platforms. By completing this section, you are ready to write a variety of workflow files – great work!

Next, we'll understand how to manage workflow runs and debug possible problems to ensure that your task runs smoothly from beginning to end.

Managing the workflow run

Now that you have learned how to create **workflow** files to trigger workflow runs, it is important to learn how you can manage them. Understanding how to view the workflow run logs, as well as rerun and cancel a workflow, will help you prepare to create test workflow runs, ensure they run as needed, and monitor them. This section will also guide you through debugging failed runs in case you need to quickly troubleshoot them and get back on track.

Visualizing a workflow run

Visual representations of script runs aren't always available on many platforms. GitHub, however, provides a real-time graph that allows you to monitor the progress of your workflow run.

To access the workflow visualization graph, click on the **Actions** tab within your repository:

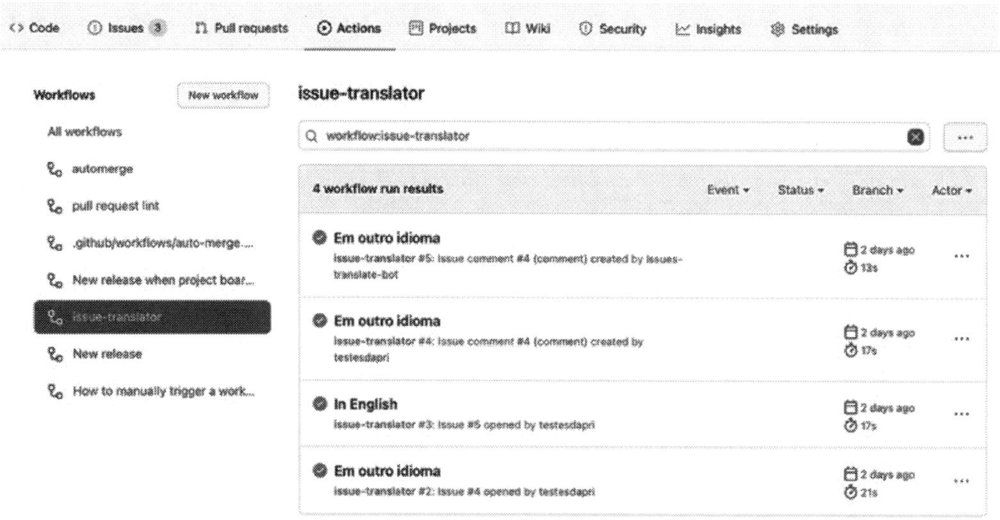

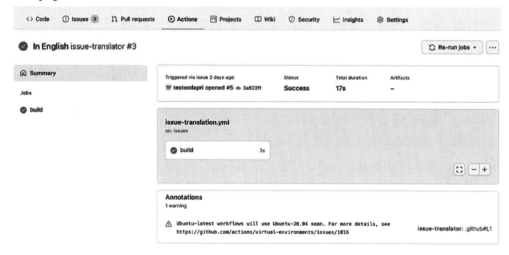

Figure 3.7 – Workflow run visualization graph

This page shows all the workflows that have run within your repository. The preceding screenshot shows results that are specific to the **issue-translator** workflow. You can see details about a different workflow by clicking on the workflow on the left-hand side, under **Workflows**.

From this page, you can also click on the workflow run itself to see details about each job within that workflow. In this example, clicking on the **In English** workflow run will show a new page:

Figure 3.8 – A view of the job within the "In English" run

From this page, you can select the **build** job to see the job's log:

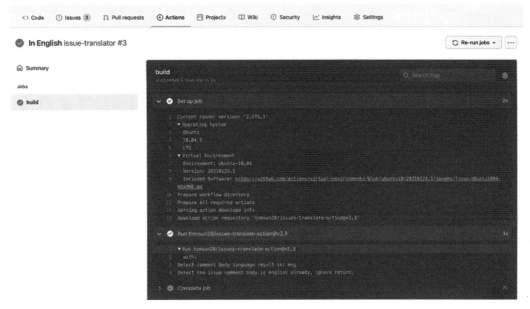

Figure 3.9 – A view of the "build" job log

The preceding screenshots also show the **Re-run jobs** button. You can rerun a job, which will use the same GITHUB_SHA and GITHUB_REF of the original event that triggered the workflow run.

Workflow run logs

The preceding screenshot shows the log for a job that ran successfully. Although the preceding screenshot shows a job that has been completed, you can see each step of the job in real time, as it progresses. This view is helpful for a number of reasons: you can see whether the job was completed successfully or if it failed. If it failed, you can see details that explain what caused the failure.

You can also use the search bar shown in the preceding screenshot to search for specific steps within that job.

> **Important note**
> Read access to the repository is required to search the log.

The following screenshot shows the log for a failed run. Note the details provided, which help explain why the run failed:

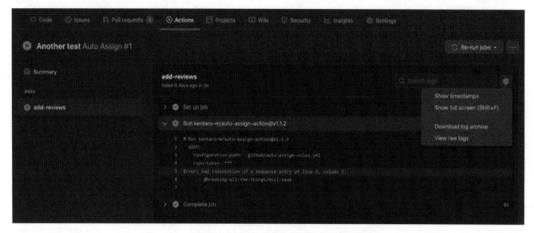

Figure 3.10 – A failed job and the error's details

The preceding screenshot also shows that it is possible to download the log archive by clicking on the settings button in the right-hand corner. This can be useful if you need to keep local records of workflow runs.

If you need more information than what is provided in the workflow run logs, you can enable two additional debug logging options. Let's take a look at them.

Runner diagnostic logging

Enable **runner diagnostic logging** to access additional information about how a runner is executing a job. When you enable this option, two extra log files will be added to the log archive: the worker process log and the runner process log.

To enable **runner diagnostic logging**, follow these steps:

1. Navigate to the **Settings** tab of the repository that contains the workflow.
2. Then, create a secret called ACTIONS_RUNNER_DEBUG and set its value to true:

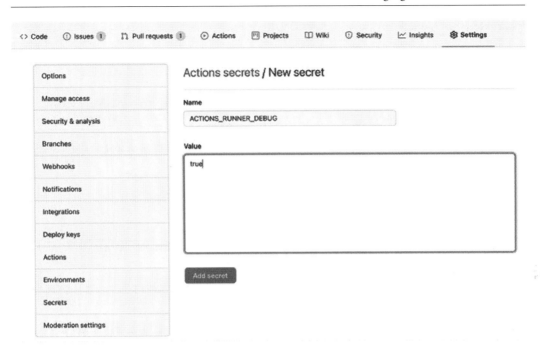

Figure 3.11 – Enabling runner diagnostic logging

Next, download the log archive for that workflow run, as shown in *Figure 3.10*. The runner process log and the worker process log will be included in the download, as shown in the following screenshot:

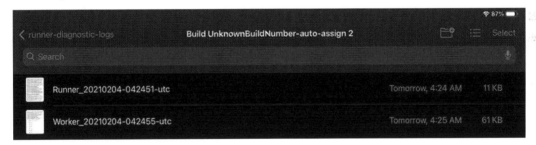

Figure 3.12 – Runner and worker log files

Step debug logging

If you need more details about a job's execution, you can enable **step debug logging**. Enabling it is similar to enabling **runner diagnostic logging**:

1. Navigate to the **Settings** tab of the repository that contains the workflow.

2. Then, create a secret called `ACTIONS_STEP_DEBUG` and set its value to `true`.

    Once step debug logging has been enabled, more debug events will be shown in the step logs when you access the logs by clicking on the **Actions** tab within your repository.

Great work! You have reached the end of *Chapter 3, A Closer Look at Workflows*. By now, you have progressed your GitHub Actions skills and are ready to advance to more complex topics that will be covered later in *Chapter 5, Writing Your Own Actions*.

Summary

In this chapter, you deepened your knowledge of workflows. You navigated through several examples that showed how webhook events can trigger GitHub Actions workflows. You also learned about the many ways keys can be used in a workflow file to authenticate it, such as `GITHUB_TOKEN` and PATs. You wrote more complex workflows using contexts and expressions.

Finally, you read about workflow run logs, and you performed the steps to enable additional debugging, which will help you manage your workflow runs and debug any failures you may come across.

With the skills you have gathered from this chapter, you are ready to start practicing and creating workflow files to help automate everyday tasks. These skills will be very convenient when you dig into *Chapter 5, Writing your Own Actions*, which will guide you in creating actions from scratch.

4
Working with Self-Hosted Runners

While GitHub offers the option to run jobs on GitHub-hosted runners, hosting your own runners can be an important advantage if your workflows demand highly customized environments.

In *Chapter 3, A Closer Look at Workflows*, you learned that GitHub Actions workflows can be as simple or as robust as you need them to be. You reviewed many examples of **webhook** events that trigger workflows, which illustrated how workflows can be used in the most diverse scenarios, such as translating **issues** or creating releases. Similarly, by using **self-hosted runners**, you can create **virtual machines (VMs)** or use hosts that will be as modest or as powerful as you need them to be while hosting the GitHub Actions runner application.

The skills you will learn in this chapter will allow you to understand the pros and cons of using a self-hosted runner when compared to using a GitHub-hosted runner. You will also see how to install the runner application, as well as build a workflow to run a job that uses a newly created self-hosted runner.

Once your self-hosted runner has been created, you will learn how to manage it, including removing it when it is no longer needed.

The following sections will guide you through this chapter:

- Creating a self-hosted runner
- Configuring a job that runs on a self-hosted runner
- Managing a self-hosted runner

Technical requirements

Self-hosted runners are, as the name suggests, self-hosted. This means you will need to have your own environment where you will install the **runner application**.

You should have access to a machine where you have permission to install applications and packages. This machine can be physical—such as a laptop, for example—or virtual; for example, a VM hosted on a hypervisor such as **Amazon Web Services** (**AWS**), VMware, or others.

By the end of this chapter, you will be able to decide whether self-hosted runners are the best alternative for your workflow. If they are, by reading this chapter, you will have acquired knowledge needed to install the runner application on a host machine and use the self-hosted runner to run a job from a workflow. Finally, you will also have the know-how to manage the self-hosted runner, review logs, and monitor its real-time activity.

Creating a self-hosted runner

The workflow examples used in previous chapters include jobs that ran on GitHub-hosted runners. As you read in *Chapter 2*, *Deep Diving into GitHub Actions*, GitHub-hosted runners can be convenient because GitHub maintains the VMs built to host those runners. However, those virtual environments are built using specific hardware and software.

If your workflows require a different architecture, GitHub-hosted runners will likely not be suitable. For example, if you run jobs that demand higher amounts of memory or processing power, you can build a host machine with those specifications to host the runner application. If your workflow requires tests to be run on operating systems unsupported by GitHub-hosted runners, or if you need to use packages, tools, or software installed in your network, self-hosting the GitHub Actions runner application can be a great option. You can use a host machine that is physical or virtual, hosted on-premises, in containers, or in the cloud.

To help you learn more about what you will need to use self-hosted runners, the next few pages will show an overview of self-hosted runners, the architecture and software supported by self-hosted runners, and instructions on how to add the GitHub Actions runner application to your repository to use with a workflow.

Overview

The following screenshot summarizes the differences between self-hosted runners and GitHub-hosted runners:

	GitHub-hosted runner	Self-hosted runner
Automatic operating system updates	Yes	No
Automatic updates for software, pre-installed packages, and GitHub Actions runner application	Yes	Automatic updates to the GitHub Actions runner application only
Managed and maintained by GitHub	Yes	No
Fresh VM is created for every job execution	Yes	No
Customizable to your specific hardware, software, and security requirements	No	Yes
Free to use	Yes, with limitations	While there are no costs on the GitHub side, the user is responsible for any costs that may apply, depending on the hosting platform

The information in the preceding table shows how self-hosted runners can be highly customizable. However, note that you are responsible for maintaining the host machine. This includes software and security updates, as well as any costs included in building and hosting the environment.

Each GitHub-hosted runner is a clean, isolated VM that is destroyed when the job run is completed. This is a security feature offered by GitHub. Since this is not a feature of self-hosted runners, you will need to pay special attention to certain security risks and plan accordingly.

> **Important note**
>
> To avoid security vulnerabilities with self-hosted runners, it is recommended that you do not use them with public repositories. When your public repository is forked and a pull request is created from that fork against your repository, a workflow can be triggered that runs malicious code in your virtual environment, which may damage your host machine and network.

Now that you have had a glimpse at some of the benefits that self-hosted runners have, review the list provided next of the supported architecture and operating systems before setting out to create a host machine.

Architecture and operating systems supported by self-hosted runners

There are a variety of processor architectures and operating systems that are supported by self-hosted runners, outlined as follows:

- **Architecture**:

    ARM32—Linux

    ARM64—Linux

    x64—Linux, macOS, and Windows

- **Operating systems**:

    macOS 10.13 or later

    Windows 7 64-bit

    Windows 8.1 64-bit

    Windows 10 64-bit

    Windows Server 2012 R2 64-bit

    Windows Server 2016 64-bit

    Windows Server 2019 64-bit

Red Hat Enterprise Linux 7 (RHEL 7)

CentOS 7

Oracle Linux 7

Fedora 29 or later

Debian 9 or later

Ubuntu 16.04 or later

Linux Mint 18 or later

openSUSE 15 or later

SUSE Linux Enterprise Server (SLES) 12 SP2 or later

- **Requirements**: Once you decide which operating system you will use to host the GitHub Actions runner application, make sure the machine meets the following requirements:

  - **Hardware power**: While the GitHub Actions runner application has modest operating resource requirements, ensure the host machine is provisioned accordingly with the resources required by the types of jobs that will be created.

  - **Supported operating system**: Choose a supported operating system and install the GitHub Actions runner application.

Communication with GitHub

The host machine must have a connection with GitHub, as well as network access to the following **Uniform Resource Locators (URLs)**:

- `github.com`
- `api.github.com`
- `*.actions.githubusercontent.com`
- `codeload.github.com`
- `github-releases.githubusercontent.com`

Adding the GitHub Actions runner application to your repository

Considering that you have provisioned a macOS, Linux, or Windows environment to host the runner application (the steps on how to create a host machine are out of the scope of this book), you can use the following instructions to add a self-hosted runner to your repository:

1. Navigate to your repository main page and click on the **Settings** tab.

2. Then, click on the **Actions** option on the left-hand-side menu, as illustrated in the following screenshot:

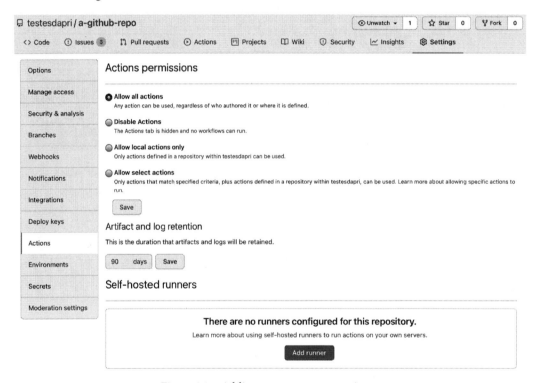

Figure 4.1 – Adding a runner to a repository

3. Click on **Add runner**.

4. Select the operating system and architecture of the machine you will use to host the runner application.

5. Follow the instructions on the screen, as illustrated in the following screenshot:

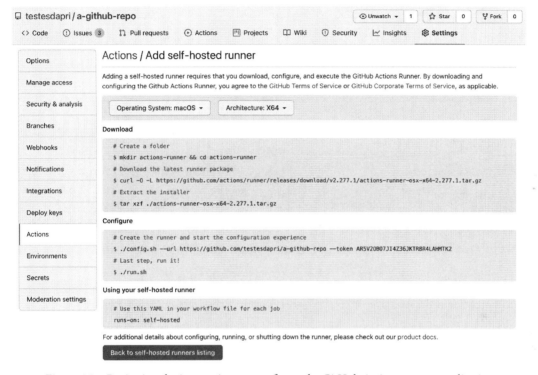

Figure 4.2 – Reviewing the instructions to configure the GitHub Actions runner application

6. Next, review the steps being followed on a macOS machine.

    Create a folder and download the latest runner package, as illustrated in the following screenshot:

```
testesdapri ~/Desktop: $ mkdir actions-runner && cd actions-runner
testesdapri ~/Desktop/actions-runner: $ curl -o actions-runner-osx-x64-2.278.0.tar.gz -L https://
github.com/actions/runner/releases/download/v2.278.0/actions-runner-osx-x64-2.278.0.tar.gz
  % Total    % Received % Xferd  Average Speed   Time    Time     Time  Current
                                 Dload  Upload   Total   Spent    Left  Speed
100   645  100   645    0     0    244      0  0:00:02  0:00:02 --:--:--   244
100 48.7M  100 48.7M    0     0   2106k      0  0:00:23  0:00:23 --:--:--  2036k
```

Figure 4.3 – Using the macOS terminal to download the runner application

7. Extract the installer and list the files and directories downloaded, as illustrated in the following screenshot:

```
testesdapri ~/Desktop/actions-runner: $ tar xzf ./actions-runner-osx-x64-2.277.1.tar.gz
testesdapri ~/Desktop/actions-runner: $ ls -l
total 100776
-rw-r--r--    1 talktopri  staff  51126670 Feb 27 22:50 actions-runner-osx-x64-2.277.1.tar.gz
drwxr-xr-x  231 talktopri  staff      7392 Feb  9 13:51 bin
-rwxr-xr-x    1 talktopri  staff      2452 Feb  9 13:49 config.sh
-rwxr-xr-x    1 talktopri  staff       646 Feb  9 13:49 env.sh
drwxr-xr-x    3 talktopri  staff        96 Feb  9 13:50 externals
-rwxr-xr-x    1 talktopri  staff      1598 Feb  9 13:49 run.sh
```

Figure 4.4 – Listing the downloaded files and directories

8. Create the runner, start the configuration, and run it.

The `config.sh` script run during this step requires the destination URL—note in this example that the URL is the repository's URL: `https://github.com/testesdapri/a-github-repo`. The script also accepts a time-sensitive, automatically generated token (the following screenshot shows the first few characters of the token, starting with AR5V). When you hit *Enter* to run the script, you will be prompted to enter a few options. The first one is the name of the runner. In this example, the name used is `testesdapri-runner`.

You can also create labels during this step. To learn more about creating and assigning labels, see the *Creating labels and assigning them to self-hosted runners* section.

You can see the runner application being configured and run in the following screenshot:

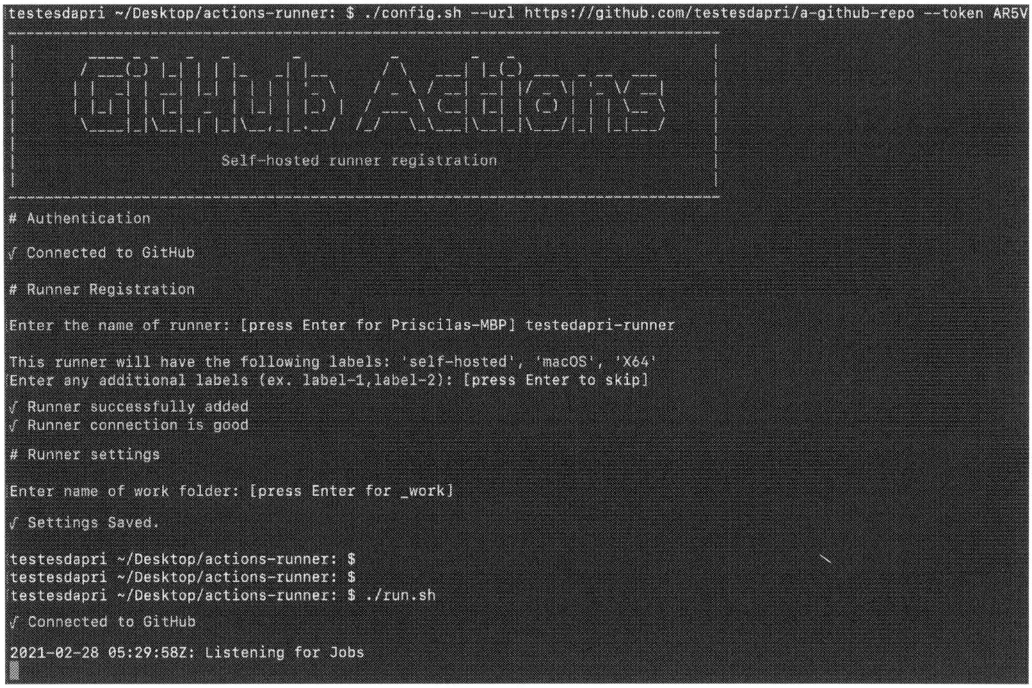

Figure 4.5 – Configuring and running the runner application

The `Listening for Jobs` output you can see in the preceding screenshot confirms that the script ran successfully. It also signals that the self-hosted runner is ready to be used in a workflow. To verify that the runner has also been added on the GitHub side, navigate to your repository's **Settings** page.

This is what you should see:

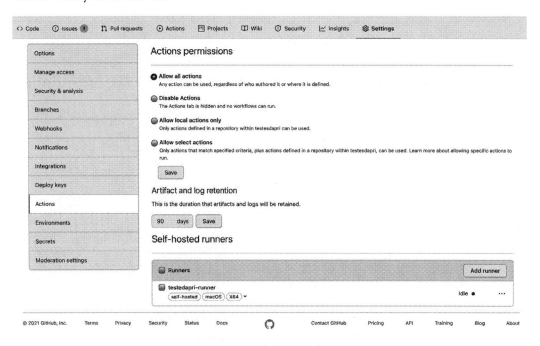

Figure 4.6 – The runner has been added to your repository

Well done! You have added your first self-hosted runner to your GitHub repository.

Next, the following sections will guide you through how to configure the runner application as a service, and how to create labels and assign them to a self-hosted runner. Although these skills are not required to start using self-hosted runners in your workflow, they will save you time when managing several runners.

Setting the self-hosted runner to run as a service

Follow these steps if you would like the GitHub Actions runner application to start the runner application when the host machine starts.

> **Important note**
> The following instructions are run on a macOS machine. If you are using a Linux or Windows operating system, you can find instructions on GitHub's official documentation page: `https://docs.github.com/en/actions/hosting-your-own-runners/configuring-the-self-hosted-runner-application-as-a-service`.

Open the terminal and follow these steps:

1. Stop the self-hosted runner application, if it is running. You can use the *Ctrl + Z* keys on your keyboard to do this.

2. Install the service by running ./svc.sh install, as illustrated in the following screenshot:

```
testesdapri ~/Desktop/actions-runner: $ ./svc.sh install
Creating launch runner in /Users/talktopri/Library/LaunchAgents/actions.runner.testesdapri-a-github-repo.testedapri-runner.plist
Creating /Users/talktopri/Library/Logs/actions.runner.testesdapri-a-github-repo.testedapri-runner
Creating /Users/talktopri/Library/LaunchAgents/actions.runner.testesdapri-a-github-repo.testedapri-runner.plist
Creating runsvc.sh
Creating .service
svc install complete
```

Figure 4.7 – Installing the service

3. Start the service with ./svc.sh start, as illustrated in the following screenshot:

```
testesdapri ~/Desktop/actions-runner: $ ./svc.sh start
starting actions.runner.testesdapri-a-github-repo.testedapri-runner
status actions.runner.testesdapri-a-github-repo.testedapri-runner:

/Users/talktopri/Library/LaunchAgents/actions.runner.testesdapri-a-github-repo.testedapri-runner.plist

Started:
62978 0 actions.runner.testesdapri-a-github-repo.testedapri-runner
```

Figure 4.8 – Starting the service

4. Check the status of the service with ./svc.sh status, as illustrated in the following screenshot:

```
testesdapri ~/Desktop/actions-runner: $ ./svc.sh status
status actions.runner.testesdapri-a-github-repo.testedapri-runner:

/Users/talktopri/Library/LaunchAgents/actions.runner.testesdapri-a-github-repo.testedapri-runner.plist

Started:
- 126 actions.runner.testesdapri-a-github-repo.testedapri-runner
```

Figure 4.9 – Verifying the service status

5. Stop the service with ./svc.sh stop, as illustrated in the following screenshot:

```
testesdapri ~/Desktop/actions-runner: $ ./svc.sh stop
stopping actions.runner.testesdapri-a-github-repo.testedapri-runner
status actions.runner.testesdapri-a-github-repo.testedapri-runner:

/Users/talktopri/Library/LaunchAgents/actions.runner.testesdapri-a-github-repo.testedapri-runner.plist

Stopped
```

Figure 4.10 – Stopping the service

6. Uninstall the service with `./svc.sh uninstall`, as illustrated in the following screenshot:

```
testesdapri ~/Desktop/actions-runner: $ ./svc.sh uninstall
uninstalling actions.runner.testesdapri-a-github-repo.testedapri-runner
stopping actions.runner.testesdapri-a-github-repo.testedapri-runner
/Users/talktopri/Library/LaunchAgents/actions.runner.testesdapri-a-github-repo.testedapri-runner.plist: Could not find specified service
status actions.runner.testesdapri-a-github-repo.testedapri-runner:

/Users/talktopri/Library/LaunchAgents/actions.runner.testesdapri-a-github-repo.testedapri-runner.plist

Stopped

testesdapri ~/Desktop/actions-runner: $ ./svc.sh status
status actions.runner.testesdapri-a-github-repo.testedapri-runner:

not installed
```

Figure 4.11 – Uninstalling the service

You have just learned how to install, manage, and uninstall the runner application as a service. Next, see how you can organize your self-hosted runner by using labels.

Creating labels and assigning them to self-hosted runners

Labels can be used to identify a runner. When you are ready to use self-hosted runners in workflows, labels can be a helpful option to add to the workflow `.yml` file to specify which runner a job must use.

There are two different ways to create labels and associate them with your self-hosted runner, outlined as follows:

- Using the configuration script
- Using the GitHub web interface

Using the configuration script is simple. When you first use the `./config.sh` script to configure the GitHub Actions runner application, you are prompted to enter the name of the runner and any additional labels, as illustrated in the following screenshot:

```
√ Connected to GitHub

# Runner Registration

Enter the name of runner: [press Enter for Priscilas-MBP] testesdapri-runner

This runner will have the following labels: 'self-hosted', 'macOS', 'X64'
Enter any additional labels (ex. label-1,label-2): [press Enter to skip] dev-runner

√ Runner successfully added
√ Runner connection is good

# Runner settings
```

Figure 4.12 – Using the configuration script to create labels

The preceding screenshot shows how the name `testesdapri-runner` was entered for the name of the runner, and a `dev-runner` label was created.

You can also verify that a label has been created and applied to your runner by navigating to your repository's **Settings** page. Notice how the following screenshot shows the `dev-runner` label applied to the `testesdapri-runner` runner:

Figure 4.13 – A label was created and assigned to the runner using the ./config.sh script

Alternatively, you can create and assign labels to self-hosted runners by using GitHub's web interface, as follows:

1. Navigate to your repository's **Settings** page. Then, click on the **Actions** item on the left-hand-side menu.

2. On the list of runners, click on the upside-down triangle next to the labels. This will open a text field, where you enter the name of your new label.

The following screenshot shows how the `javascript-tools` label was created:

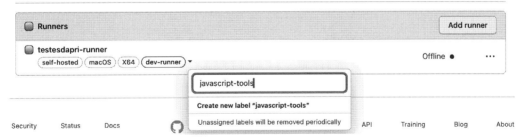

Figure 4.14 – A javascript-tools label was created and assigned to the runner using the web interface

You have learned how to add a self-hosted runner to your repository, as well as how to create and assign labels to those runners. Labels allow you to send jobs to self-hosted runners that are labeled according to their operating system, architecture, or environment, for example. Labels will be helpful in the next section, where you will read about passing a self-hosted runner to the `runs-on` key of your workflow.

Configuring a job that runs on a self-hosted runner

Similarly to GitHub-hosted runners, self-hosted runners use the `runs-on` key within a workflow file. Therefore, you will use a line like the following one in your `.yml` file:

```
runs-on: [self-hosted, macOS, dev-runner]
```

Self-hosted runners automatically receive a `self-hosted` label, as well as a label to indicate the operating system and architecture you selected when you were creating a self-hosted runner on your repository's **Settings** page. In the previous example, `macOS` is the label automatically generated for the operating system. An architecture label is not being used in this case. Note how `dev-runner`, a label created using the `./config.sh` script, was also used.

The following example is of a workflow used in *Chapter 3*, *A Closer Look at Workflows*, to translate issues and issue comments that were written in a language different from English, and this workflow ran on a GitHub-hosted runner. The following code snippet shows how it was edited to use a self-hosted runner:

```
name: issue-translator

on:
  issues:
    types: [opened]
  issue_comment:
    types: [created]

jobs:
  build:
    runs-on: [self-hosted, macOS, dev-runner]
    steps:
      - uses: tomsun28/issues-translate-action@v2.3
```

A new issue was created in the repository. It was written using Portuguese, which triggered a workflow run, as you can see here in the **Actions** tab:

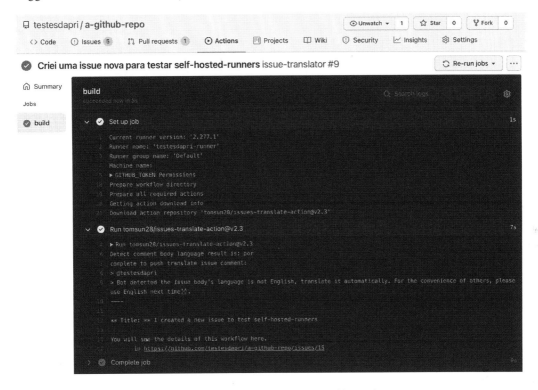

Figure 4.15 – A workflow run using a self-hosted runner

Note how the `testesdapri-runner` self-hosted runner, created following the instructions in this chapter, was used. In the following screenshot, you can also see evidence of a job being run on the self-hosted runner host machine console:

```
√ Connected to GitHub

2021-03-01 00:42:25Z: Listening for Jobs
2021-03-01 00:43:13Z: Running job: build
2021-03-01 00:43:29Z: Job build completed with result: Succeeded
2021-03-01 00:43:35Z: Running job: build
2021-03-01 00:43:50Z: Job build completed with result: Succeeded
```

Figure 4.16 – Real-time information about a job being run can be seen on the host machine console

While the workflow run example in this section completed successfully, it is possible that you will need to troubleshoot job builds that run on your self-hosted runner application. Read on to the next section to learn more about reviewing logs and managing self-hosted runners.

Managing a self-hosted runner

Self-hosted runners are unique because they require more maintenance from the host machine administrator. While you may have access to the host machine's logs and other monitoring tools, it is also important to manage and monitor the GitHub Actions runner application.

This section will guide you in understanding the status of self-hosted runners, reviewing job logs and runner log files, understanding the runner application's automatic update process, and removing a self-hosted runner that will no longer be needed.

By the end of this section, you will have gathered the skills necessary to create, use, and manage a self-hosted runner successfully.

Understanding the status of self-hosted runners

You can review the status of self-hosted runners by navigating to the **Settings** page of your repository, and then clicking on **Actions** on the left-hand-side menu. The page that comes up will list the runners that have been added to your repository.

Note how the runner may be displaying a status of either **Active**, **Idle**, or **Offline**, outlined as follows:

- **Active**: The runner is currently executing a job. This status is illustrated in the following screenshot:

Figure 4.17 – The status of this runner is Active

- **Idle**: The runner is ready to execute jobs. An **Idle** status also indicates that the runner is connected to GitHub. This status is illustrated in the following screenshot:

Figure 4.18 – The status of this runner is Idle

- **Offline**: The runner is not connected to GitHub. There are a few reasons why a runner can be offline: the runner application is not running, the runner application cannot communicate with GitHub, or the host machine is offline. This status is illustrated in the following screenshot:

Figure 4.19 – The status of this runner is Offline

While understanding the definitions for each runner status is helpful, you may need more information to diagnose why a runner is unexpectedly offline, for example. The next section will show you where worker and runner logs are located. You will also learn what kind of information is recorded in those files.

Reviewing logs

Each workflow job processed by the runner application is recorded in a detailed log file. Similarly, the self-hosted runner application statuses and activities are written to a separate set of files. Analyzing both sets of log files can be helpful if you need to diagnose issues or troubleshoot problems.

Job log files

These files contain details about each workflow job processed by the runner and are stored in your self-hosted runner's `_diag` directory. All job log filenames start with `Worker_`, as can be seen in the following screenshot:

```
testesdapri ~/Desktop/actions-runner: $ ls -l
total 101584
drwxr-xr-x    7 talktopri  staff      224 Feb 28 19:48 _diag
drwxr-xr-x    7 talktopri  staff      224 Feb 28 19:48 _work
-rw-r--r--    1 talktopri  staff 51126670 Feb 28 19:45 actions-runner-osx-x64-2.277.1.tar.gz
drwxr-xr-x  231 talktopri  staff     7392 Feb  9 13:51 bin
-rwxr-xr-x    1 talktopri  staff     2452 Feb  9 13:49 config.sh
-rwxr-xr-x    1 talktopri  staff      646 Feb  9 13:49 env.sh
drwxr-xr-x    3 talktopri  staff       96 Feb  9 13:50 externals
-rwxr-xr-x    1 talktopri  staff     1598 Feb  9 13:49 run.sh
-rwxr-xr-x    1 talktopri  staff     3276 Feb 28 19:46 svc.sh
testesdapri ~/Desktop/actions-runner: $ ls -l _diag/
total 344
-rw-r--r--    1 talktopri  staff    18461 Feb 28 19:46 Runner_20210301-014601-utc.log
-rw-r--r--    1 talktopri  staff    16912 Feb 28 19:48 Runner_20210301-014642-utc.log
-rw-r--r--    1 talktopri  staff    63977 Feb 28 19:47 Worker_20210301-014741-utc.log
-rw-r--r--    1 talktopri  staff    69201 Feb 28 19:48 Worker_20210301-014804-utc.log
drwxr-xr-x    2 talktopri  staff       64 Feb 28 19:48 pages
```

Figure 4.20 – Viewing the contents of the /actions-runner/_diag directory on the host machine

Job log files are usually longer than runner log files. They carry thousands of lines that record every step of each job, as well as its status. The following screenshot shows a few lines of a job log file, illustrating a job that was successfully completed:

```
[2021-03-01 01:47:51Z INFO JobExtension] Initialize Env context
[2021-03-01 01:47:51Z INFO JobExtension] Initialize steps context
[2021-03-01 01:47:51Z INFO JobExtension] Total accessible running process: 341.
[2021-03-01 01:47:51Z INFO JobRunner] Job result after all job steps finish: Succeeded
[2021-03-01 01:47:51Z INFO JobRunner] Completing the job execution context.
[2021-03-01 01:47:51Z INFO JobRunner] Shutting down the job server queue.
[2021-03-01 01:47:51Z INFO JobServerQueue] Fire signal to shutdown all queues.
[2021-03-01 01:47:51Z INFO JobServerQueue] All queue process task stopped.
```

Figure 4.21 – Reviewing the contents of a Worker_ file

The next category of log files is stored in the same directory as job log files.

Runner application log files

Similar to job log files, runner application log files are stored in the `_diag` directory. These filenames start with `Runner_` and record information about the runner application every time it is started, as the following screenshot shows:

```
[2021-03-01 01:46:02Z INFO Terminal] WRITE LINE:
[2021-03-01 01:46:02Z INFO Terminal] WRITE LINE: ----------------------------------------
[2021-03-01 01:46:02Z INFO Terminal] WRITE LINE: |
[2021-03-01 01:46:02Z INFO Terminal] WRITE LINE: |
[2021-03-01 01:46:02Z INFO Terminal] WRITE LINE: |
[2021-03-01 01:46:02Z INFO Terminal] WRITE LINE: |
[2021-03-01 01:46:02Z INFO Terminal] WRITE LINE: |
[2021-03-01 01:46:02Z INFO Terminal] WRITE LINE: |
[2021-03-01 01:46:02Z INFO Terminal] WRITE: |
[2021-03-01 01:46:02Z INFO Terminal] WRITE: Self-hosted runner registration
[2021-03-01 01:46:02Z INFO Terminal] WRITE LINE: |
[2021-03-01 01:46:02Z INFO Terminal] WRITE LINE: |
[2021-03-01 01:46:02Z INFO Terminal] WRITE LINE: ----------------------------------------
[2021-03-01 01:46:02Z INFO ConfigurationManager] ConfigureAsync
[2021-03-01 01:46:02Z INFO ConfigurationStore] IsConfigured()
[2021-03-01 01:46:02Z INFO ConfigurationStore] IsConfigured: False
[2021-03-01 01:46:02Z INFO ConfigurationManager] Is configured: False
[2021-03-01 01:46:02Z INFO CommandSettings] Arg 'url': 'https://github.com/testesdapri/a-github-repo'
[2021-03-01 01:46:02Z INFO CommandSettings] Remove url from Arg dictionary.
[2021-03-01 01:46:02Z INFO CommandSettings] Arg 'token': '***'
[2021-03-01 01:46:02Z INFO CommandSettings] Remove token from Arg dictionary.
[2021-03-01 01:46:03Z INFO ConfigurationManager] Http response code: OK from 'POST https://api.github.com/actions/runner-registration'
[2021-03-01 01:46:04Z INFO ConfigurationManager] cred retrieved via GitHub auth
[2021-03-01 01:46:04Z INFO RunnerServer] Establish connection with 100 seconds timeout.
[2021-03-01 01:46:04Z INFO GitHubActionsService] Starting operation Location.GetConnectionData
[2021-03-01 01:46:04Z INFO RunnerServer] Establish connection with 60 seconds timeout.
[2021-03-01 01:46:04Z INFO GitHubActionsService] Starting operation Location.GetConnectionData
[2021-03-01 01:46:04Z INFO RunnerServer] Establish connection with 60 seconds timeout.
[2021-03-01 01:46:04Z INFO GitHubActionsService] Starting operation Location.GetConnectionData
[2021-03-01 01:46:04Z INFO GitHubActionsService] Finished operation Location.GetConnectionData
[2021-03-01 01:46:05Z INFO GitHubActionsService] Finished operation Location.GetConnectionData
[2021-03-01 01:46:05Z INFO GitHubActionsService] Finished operation Location.GetConnectionData
[2021-03-01 01:46:05Z INFO Terminal] WRITE LINE:
[2021-03-01 01:46:05Z INFO ConfigurationManager] Test Connection complete.
```

Figure 4.22 – Reviewing the contents of a Runner_ file

While `Runner_` files are often smaller in size when compared to `Worker_` files, they can be instrumental in troubleshooting issues that can be related to the version of the runner application or to problems that could have happened during the automatic update process.

The automatic update process

While you are responsible for managing and maintaining the host environment (including the operating system, pre-installed packages, security packages, and so on), GitHub updates the runner application automatically. While no manual intervention is needed during these automatic updates, it is recommended that you monitor this process. This can help you identify possible update issues early on and stay informed about each update process.

You can find information about the automatic update process in the `_diag/Runner_` log files, as well as in the `_diag/SelfUpdate` log files.

Removing a self-hosted runner

If you no longer want to maintain the host machine or if you need to reuse the machine for a different project, you can easily remove a self-hosted runner from your repository.

> **Important note**
> This is a procedure that will permanently remove the self-hosted runner from your repository. You may want to consider stopping the runner instead. You can stop the runner by turning off the host machine or stopping the `run` application on the host machine.

To remove a self-hosted runner, follow these instructions:

1. Navigate to your repository's **Settings** page.
2. Then, click on the **Actions** item on the left-hand-side menu.
3. Identify from the list of runners the one you want to remove.
4. Click on the ellipsis on the right. Then, click on **Remove**, as illustrated in the following screenshot:

Figure 4.23 – Removing a self-hosted runner

5. Follow the instructions on the screen to remove the runner completely, using the web interface or the host machine shell prompt.

Well done—you have completed *Chapter 4, Working with Self-Hosted Runners*! You are now ready to create, use, manage, and remove self-hosted runners in your repository.

Summary

Excellent work! Now that you have completed *Chapter 4, Working with Self-Hosted Runners*, you have discovered how self-hosted runners can add flexibility and customization to your workflows. By hosting your own runner application, you can build a hosting machine and pick hardware and software that are not available for GitHub-hosted runners.

You walked through the steps of installing and configuring the runner application in your host machine.

You also revisited a workflow that previously used a GitHub-hosted runner, and recreated the job using a self-hosted runner. You practiced adding a self-hosted runner in a workflow by simply using the right key and the right labels: `runs-on: [self-hosted, macOS, dev-runner]`.

Finally, you reviewed the contents of runner and job log files, while learning how to manage and maintain self-hosted runners.

Learning about self-hosted runners gives you the flexibility to try any of the workflow examples throughout this book in your own environment. It also provides you with more tools to create the perfect workflow for your task.

Now that you have learned about self-hosted runners, you have a new tool that you can add to your **continuous integration/continuous deployment (CI/CD)** workflow. You will have the chance to use this newly gained skill in the next *Chapter 5, Writing your Own Actions*, where you will have the opportunity to write a GitHub action from scratch using JavaScript and Docker.

5
Writing Your Own Actions

At this point, you have developed all the skills needed to enable GitHub Actions on a repository and write a workflow file using **YAML Ain't Markup Language** (**YAML**). You have also practiced adding existing public actions to your workflow file. Next, you will continue exploring the multitude of ways GitHub Actions can be used by writing your own action.

Actions are specific tasks that interact with a GitHub repository. In this chapter, you will learn—among other things—that you can write custom code to create an action using JavaScript and Docker. To help you gather the information needed to create your own action, this chapter is organized into the following sections:

- Overview
- Reviewing the **metadata syntax**
- Using exit codes
- Creating a **JavaScript action**
- Creating a **Docker container action**
- Creating a **composite run steps action**

By the end of this chapter, you will be able to create your own action using different technologies. You will also have gathered knowledge to test your newly created action, to verify that all works as expected.

Technical requirements

In addition to the skills you have learned throughout the previous chapters, you will need a basic understanding of JavaScript and Docker in order to write both types of actions.

Depending on the type of action you decide to write, you will need to have `Node.js` and Docker installed on your workstation.

Overview

Types of actions

You can create three types of actions: **Docker container actions**, **JavaScript actions**, and **composite run steps actions**.

Docker container actions can be slower than JavaScript actions because an image has to be retrieved before the Docker container can be built. However, Docker containers can be especially fitting for actions that must run in specific environments for two main reasons: they allow for customization of operating systems, tools, packages and dependencies that will be installed on the container, and they ensure that the action will run reliably and consistently.

> **Important note**
> Docker container actions only support one operating system, Linux. If you are using GitHub-hosted runners, verify that you have selected Linux runners. If you are using self-hosted runners, the runner must be running on a Linux operating system and Docker must be installed.

Differently from Docker container actions, **JavaScript actions** run on the runner machine. This means that if you are using GitHub-hosted runners, for example, it is possible that any binaries that are part of the code that makes up your JavaScript action may not be compatible with all operating systems.

Although they might not be the best fit for tasks that need to run in specific environments, JavaScript actions have other benefits, such as executing faster than Docker container actions.

Composite run steps actions are not bound to a specific programming language or platform. By using composite run steps actions, you are able to combine multiple workflow run steps in one action. Composite run steps actions support Linux, macOS, and Windows.

All three types of actions share the same requirement: a metadata file written using YAML, where you can define the main entry point for your action, as well as any **inputs and outputs (I/Os)**.

Reviewing the metadata syntax

The metadata syntax required to create an action must be written using YAML. If you are not familiar with YAML, start by reading the *Introduction to YAML* section in *Chapter 1, Learning the Foundations for GitHub Actions*.

> **Important note**
> The metadata filename must be either `action.yaml` or `action.yml`.

Most elements in a YAML file are organized in key-value pairs. That format is also used in the action metadata syntax. This chapter presents a list of all **required keys** that you must add to an action metadata file, as follows:

- `name`: The name of your action, which will also be displayed in the **Actions** tab of your GitHub repository.

- `description`: A description of your action.

- `runs`: Determines the application used to run the code.

  For Docker actions, this key configures the image used for the Docker action.

  For JavaScript actions, this key configures the path to the location where the code that builds the action lives.

  For composite run steps actions, `runs` configures the path to the composite action.

- `runs.using`:

  For Docker actions, the value for this key should be set to `docker`.

  For JavaScript actions, this key needs a value to determine the application used to run the code specified in `runs.main`.

  For composite run steps actions, the value for this key should be set to `composite`.

- `runs.main` (specific to JavaScript actions): The file that contains your action code—such as `index.js`, for example.

- `runs.steps` (specific to composite run steps actions): The run steps that you want to execute in this action.

- `runs.steps[*].run` (specific to composite run steps actions): The command you want to run. The value for this key can be passed as `${{ github.action_path }}/directory/script.sh` or as `$GITHUB_ACTION_PATH/script.sh`.

- `runs.steps[*].shell` (specific to composite run steps actions): The shell you want to use to run the command. Shells such as `bash`, `powershell`, and `python` are supported. To see a list of all supported shells, see this GitHub help article: `https://docs.github.com/en/actions/reference/workflow-syntax-for-github-actions#using-a-specific-shell`.

- `runs.image` (specific to Docker container actions): The Docker image of the container the action will run in. The value for this key can be one of the following:

  The Docker base image name

  A local `Dockerfile` that lives in your repository

  A public image in a registry such as Docker Hub or GitHub Container Registry (`ghcr.io`)

> **Important note**
>
> To reference a `Dockerfile` local to your repository in your action, verify that the file is named `Dockerfile` and that you are using a path relative to your action metadata file (`action.yml` or `action.yaml`).

The following example shows part of the content in the `action.yml` file for the most used action in GitHub Marketplace—the `actions/checkout` action:

```
name: 'Checkout'
description: 'Checkout a Git repository at a particular
version'
inputs:
  repository:
    description: 'Repository name with owner. For example,
actions/checkout'
    default: ${{ github.repository }}
(...)
```

```
runs:
  using: node12
  main: dist/index.js
  post: dist/index.js
```

Note how this file includes the `name`, `description`, `runs`, `runs.using`, and `runs.main` required keys. It also uses optional keys such as `inputs`, `input.id`, `input.id.description`, `input.id.default`, and `runs.post`.

> **Important note**
>
> For a comprehensive list that includes optional keys, visit the GitHub documentation at `https://docs.github.com/en/actions/creating-actions/metadata-syntax-for-github-actions`.

While not a required addition to the metadata file, exit codes represent an important part of writing your own actions. The next section will show you how to use exit codes within your action.

Using exit codes

Adding exit codes to your action can help you monitor the action's check run status.

GitHub displays statuses to illustrate whether an action run succeeded or failed. Those statuses are binary and simply represent whether an action run succeeded or failed, and are outlined further here:

1. The action completed **successfully**—Exit status is `0` and the check run status is `success`.

2. The action **failed**—Exit status is `non-zero` (any integer) and the check run status is `failed`. All concurrent actions are cancelled, and future actions are skipped.

Adding exit codes to a JavaScript action

Use the `@actions/core` actions toolkit package to set failure exit codes and log a message, as follows:

```
try {
  // add thing to be tried here
} catch (error) {
```

```
  core.setFailed(error.message);
}
```

Adding exit codes to a Docker container action

Use your `entrypoint.sh` file to add a failure exit code, as follows:

```
if <this happens> ; then
   echo "Something went wrong"
   exit 1
fi
```

Now that you have reviewed the metadata syntax you will need to use, you are ready to learn how to write your own action. The next few sections will guide you in writing JavaScript, Docker, and composite run steps actions.

Creating a JavaScript action

The next few pages will walk you through the creation of a JavaScript action. Although basic JavaScript knowledge will be helpful in understanding parts of this section, the main goal is to provide you with knowledge needed to create an action from scratch. Focus on the code itself will be minimal.

Once you are done reading this section, you will be able to create a JavaScript action and verify that it works as intended by using it in a workflow.

Prerequisites

To follow the steps presented in this section, you will need the following:

1. A new GitHub repository. Throughout this section, the `talktopri/a-javascript-action` repository will be used.

2. A local copy of your GitHub repository. Use the `git clone` command to clone your GitHub repository to your workstation. Revisit *Chapter 1, Learning the Foundations for GitHub Actions,* if you need more details on how to accomplish that.

3. `Node.js` version 12.x. Download and install `Node.js` on your workstation.

4. A `package.json` file. Once you have `Node.js` installed on your workstation, open a shell window and, from within your GitHub repository directory, type `npm init -y` to initialize the directory, accepting all of its default values.

> **Important note**
>
> To download `Node.js`, visit `https://nodejs.org/en/download/current/`.

The following screenshot shows the GitHub repository being cloned locally. Note how the `cd` command changed the directory from `Desktop` to the repository directory, `/Desktop/a-javascript-action`. Then, the `package.json` file was generated once `npm init -y` was executed:

```
testesdapri ~/Desktop: $ git clone https://github.com/testesdapri/a-javascript-action.git
Cloning into 'a-javascript-action'...
remote: Enumerating objects: 3, done.
remote: Counting objects: 100% (3/3), done.
remote: Total 3 (delta 0), reused 0 (delta 0), pack-reused 0
Unpacking objects: 100% (3/3), done.
testesdapri ~/Desktop: $ cd a-javascript-action/
testesdapri ~/Desktop/a-javascript-action: $ npm init -y
Wrote to /Users/talktopri/Desktop/a-javascript-action/package.json:
```

Figure 5.1 – Cloning a GitHub repository and initializing a new npm package

Defining the action

Every action needs a metadata file. To start your JavaScript action, create a metadata file in the root directory of your GitHub repository, as illustrated in the following code snippet. This file will define the main entry point, as well as the I/Os for your action. The metadata file can be called either `action.yml` or `action.yaml`:

```yaml
name: "my javascript action"

description: "Simple greeting with GitHub Actions"

inputs:
  first-greeting:
    description: "who would you like to greet in the console"
    required: true
    default: "Hubot"
  second-greeting:
    description: "another person to greet"
```

```
      required: true
      default: "Mona"
    third-greeting:
      description: "a third greeting"
      required: true
      default: "Testesdapri"
    last-one-greeted:
      description: "the person greeted last"
outputs:
    last-one-greeted:
      description: "the person greeted last"
runs:
    using: "node12"
    main: "index.js"
```

This metadata file defines the I/Os and entry point for a simple `hello-world` action. Note how this file determines that three different inputs are expected (`first-greeting`, `second-greeting`, and `third-greeting`), but only `first-greeting` is *required*. Similarly, this file determines what to output: `first-one-greeted`.

> **Important note**
> While there were some modifications to its original content, the inspiration for this metadata file and the `index.js` file in this section comes from a free online GitHub Actions course that you can find in GitHub's **Learning Lab**: `https://lab.github.com/githubtraining/github-actions:-writing-javascript-actions`.

The next step is to create an `index.js` file and write the JavaScript logic that will power this action when the workflow is triggered.

Writing the action logic

If you are familiar with JavaScript, you have probably added existing packages that bring commands or libraries to help with some parts of your code. These packages are often added to a JavaScript file using a `const <name> = require("package-name");` line. In the following examples, a specific package will be used. The `@actions/core` package provides an interface to the I/O variables, as well as exit statuses.

To use this package, ensure that you have it installed by running npm install @ actions/core on the command line.

Create an index.js file in your GitHub repository and add the following content to it:

```javascript
const core = require("@actions/core");

const firstGreeting = core.getInput("first-greeting");
const secondGreeting = core.getInput("second-greeting");
const thirdGreeting = core.getInput("third-greeting");
const lastOneGreeted = core.getInput("last-one-greeted");

async function run() {
    try {
        if (firstGreeting) {
            core.setOutput("last-one-greeted", firstGreeting);
        } else if (secondGreeting) {
            core.setOutput("last-one-greeted", secondGreeting);
        } else if (thirdGreeting) {
            core.setOutput("last-one-greeted", thirdGreeting);
        }
    } catch (error) {
        core.setFailed(error.message);
    }
}

run();
console.log(`The first one to be greeted was
${firstGreeting}!`);
console.log(`The second one to be greeted was
${secondGreeting}!`);
console.log(`The last one to be greeted was
${thirdGreeting}!`);
```

Note the lines showing core.getInput. This is provided by the @actions/core toolkit and is used to receive input provided by the user.

This action will receive user input, then provide an output showing who the last greeted person was, using the `core.setOutput` package. In case of any problems or exceptions, an error message will also be displayed.

Now that both the metadata file and the logic for this JavaScript action have been written and added to the GitHub repository, it is time to test things out by creating a workflow file and triggering an action, as illustrated in the following screenshot:

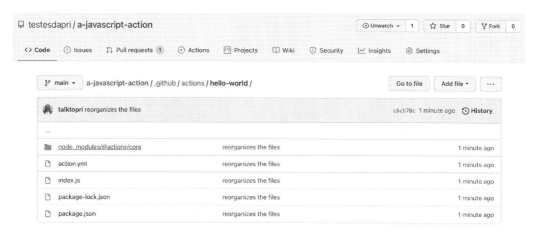

Figure 5.2 – The metadata and JavaScript files were added to the repository

Ensuring all works as expected

You have written your first JavaScript action—great work! Now, you have the opportunity to add your action to a workflow file—similar to what you accomplished in previous chapters—and ensure all works as expected.

To ensure your action works as expected, create a new workflow file in your GitHub repository. Remember that workflow files must live in the `/.github/workflows/` directory. If you need details on how to create a workflow file, visit *Chapter 2*, *Deep Diving into GitHub Actions*.

Next, paste the following content into your newly created workflow file. This will trigger a workflow run when a new `pull` request is labeled. Notice how your newly created action is passed under `steps`:

```
name: JS Actions


on:
  pull_request:
```

```
    types: [labeled]

jobs:
  action:
    runs-on: ubuntu-latest

    steps:
      - uses: actions/checkout@v1

      - name: hello-action
        uses: ./.github/actions/hello-world
```

Create a test `pull` request and add a label to it. This will trigger the following workflow run:

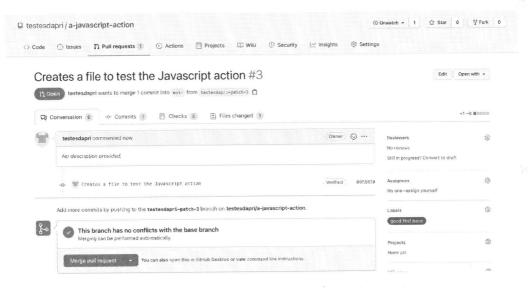

Figure 5.3 – Creating a pull request to test the JavaScript action

Then, click on the **Actions** tab. Click on the most recent workflow run, if you have multiple workflow runs in that repository, and click on **action**. That will take you to the **Action run** page, where you will be able to see each step completing successfully, as illustrated in the following screenshot:

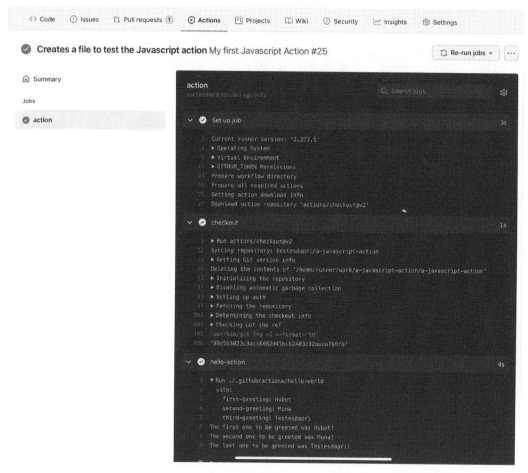

Figure 5.4 – Viewing the logs to validate that the JavaScript action ran successfully

Excellent job! The JavaScript action you created works as expected and all jobs are completed successfully.

You have mastered the first type of action that can be created in GitHub. Next, you can learn more about the second type of action that you can create from scratch: a Docker action. Review the steps needed to write a successful Docker action by reading the next section of this chapter.

Creating a Docker container action

The next few pages will walk you through the creation of a Docker container action. Although basic Docker knowledge will be helpful in understanding parts of this section, the main goal is to provide you with knowledge needed to create an action from scratch. Focus on Docker itself will be minimal.

Once you are done reading this section, you will be able to create a Docker container action and verify that it works as intended by using it in a workflow.

Prerequisites

To follow the steps presented in this section, you will need the following:

1. A new GitHub repository. Throughout this section, the `talktopri/a-docker-action` repository will be used.

2. A local copy of your GitHub repository. Use the `git clone` command to clone your GitHub repository to your workstation. Revisit *Chapter 1, Learning the Foundations for GitHub Actions,* if you need more details on how to accomplish that.

    The following screenshot shows the GitHub repository being cloned locally. Note how the `cd` command changed the directory from `Desktop` to the `/Desktop/a-docker-action` repository directory:

```
testesdapri ~/Desktop: $ git clone https://github.com/testesdapri/a-docker-action.git
Cloning into 'a-docker-action'...
remote: Enumerating objects: 3, done.
remote: Counting objects: 100% (3/3), done.
remote: Total 3 (delta 0), reused 0 (delta 0), pack-reused 0
Unpacking objects: 100% (3/3), done.
testesdapri ~/Desktop: $ cd a-docker-action/
```

Figure 5.5 – Cloning a GitHub repository

3. A self-hosted runner is installed in a Linux environment. The examples throughout this section use a self-hosted runner installed in a Linux environment, where Docker will be installed. Remember that Docker container actions only support Linux as the operating system. Review *Chapter 4, Working with Self-Hosted Runners,* to create your own self-hosted runner. If you prefer to use a GitHub-hosted runner instead, make sure to choose a flavor of Linux available on GitHub, such as Ubuntu.

The following screenshot shows an example of a runner application that has been successfully installed and now running on a Linux machine:

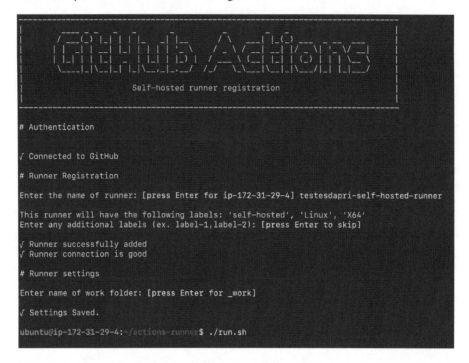

Figure 5.6 – The runner application has been installed on a Linux machine and is running

4.   Lastly, you will need to install Docker in your Linux environment, if it is not already installed. To verify that Docker is installed successfully, you can run `sudo docker run hello-world` from the command line, as follows:

```
ubuntu@ip-172-31-29-4:~$ sudo docker run hello-world
Unable to find image 'hello-world:latest' locally
latest: Pulling from library/hello-world
b8dfde127a29: Pull complete
Digest: sha256:308866a43596e83578c7dfa15e27a73011bdd402185a84c5cd7f32a88b501a24
Status: Downloaded newer image for hello-world:latest

Hello from Docker!
This message shows that your installation appears to be working correctly.
```

Figure 5.7 – Verifying that Docker is installed successfully

> **Important note**
>
> Visit `https://docs.docker.com/engine/install/` to learn how to install Docker in your environment.

Creating a Dockerfile in your GitHub repository

A `Dockerfile` is a simple text file where you can add the instructions or commands that Docker should execute.

To add a `Dockerfile` to your GitHub repository, follow these steps:

1. Create a new file called `Dockerfile` in the root of your repository, as illustrated in the following screenshot:

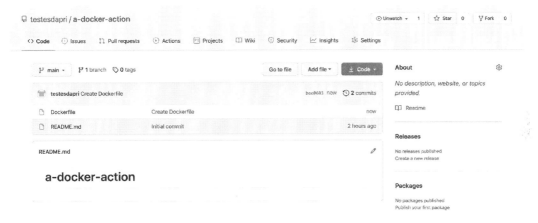

Figure 5.8 – A Dockerfile has been added to the root of the GitHub repository

2. Copy the following content and paste it into your `Dockerfile`:

```
# Container image that runs your code
FROM alpine:3.13

# Copies your code file from your action repository, like
testesdapri/a-docker-action, to the filesystem path `/` of the
container
COPY entrypoint.sh /entrypoint.sh

# Runs the command to add the execute permission to the
entrypoint.sh
RUN chmod +x entrypoint.sh

# Code file to execute when the Docker container starts up
ENTRYPOINT ["/entrypoint.sh"]
```

Note how the `Dockerfile` will also adjust the permission to the `entrypoint.sh` file. This step is very important and you will likely see a `permission denied` error when your workflow runs if you do not add it to your `Dockerfile`.

Defining the action

Every action needs a metadata file. To start your Docker action, create a metadata file within your GitHub repository, as illustrated in the following code snippet. This file will define the main entry point for your action. The metadata file can be called either `action.yml` or `action.yaml`:

```
name: "My Docker action"

description: 'Simply running a bash command and showing the
time it executed'

runs:
  using: "docker"
  main: "Dockerfile"
```

While this specific example does not include any I/Os, you can add them as needed in your workflow.

The next step is to create an `entrypoint.sh` file and write the Bash script that will power this action when the workflow is triggered.

Writing the action logic

The Bash script in the following example was kept simple on purpose. Keeping this script simple will allow you to understand the logic of this Docker action, without requiring prior experience of using Bash.

To create logic for this Docker action, create an `entrypoint.sh` file in your repository. Then, add the following content to it, which will greet the user who triggered the workflow and print the current date and time to the screen:

```
#!/bin/sh -l

echo "Hello $GITHUB_ACTOR! The time now is $(date)"
```

The first line, #!/bin/sh, indicates that the file will be executed using the Bourne shell or another compatible shell. The -l flag is for a login shell, which means that it will read and execute commands from the /etc/profile file if it exists.

Next, echo is used to print an output to the screen.

$GITHUB_ACTOR is a context and uses the username of the user who initiated the workflow run. For more details about GitHub context and expressions, review *Chapter 3, A Closer Look at Workflows*.

Lastly, $(date) is a shell command that displays the current date and time.

> **Important note**
> To learn more about Bash and other shells, you can use interactive shell tutorials, such as learnshell.org.

You have written your first Docker action—great work! Now, you have the opportunity to add your action to a workflow file—similar to what you accomplished in previous chapters—and ensure all works as expected.

Ensuring all works as expected

To ensure your action works as expected, create a new workflow file in your GitHub repository. Remember that workflow files must live in the /.github/workflows/ directory. If you need details on how to create a workflow file, visit *Chapter 2, Deep Diving into GitHub Actions*.

Next, paste the following content into your newly created workflow file. This will trigger a workflow run when an issue is opened, edited, or labeled. Notice how this workflow is using a self-hosted runner. Also, note how your newly created action is passed under steps:

```
name: A simple Docker action

on:
  issues:
    types: [opened, edited, labeled]

jobs:
  user-and-time:
    runs-on: self-hosted
```

```
name: Running a simple BASH script
steps:
- name: A simple BASH script
  id: BASH
  uses: testesdapri/a-docker-action@main
```

To trigger a workflow run, open a new issue, as illustrated in the following screenshot:

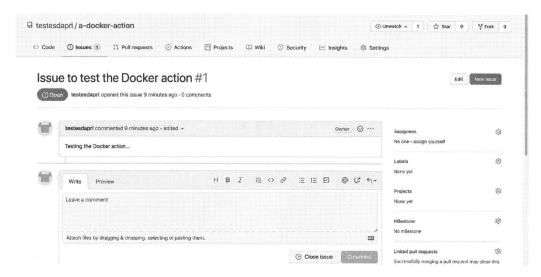

Figure 5.9 – Opening an issue to test the Docker action

Then, click on the **Actions** tab. Click on the most recent workflow run, if you have multiple workflow runs in that repository, and click on **action**. That will take you to the **Action run** page, where you will be able to see each step completing successfully, as illustrated in the following screenshot:

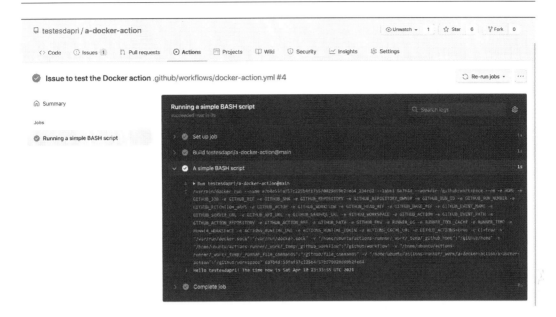

Figure 5.10 – Viewing the logs to validate that the Docker action ran successfully

Excellent job! The Docker action you created works as expected and all jobs are completed successfully.

You have mastered two of the three types of actions that can be created in GitHub. Next, you will learn more about **composite run steps** actions.

Creating a composite run steps action

The next few pages will walk you through the creation of a **composite run steps** action. This type of action is not bound to a specific programming language or platform. Composite run steps actions are unique because they allow you to combine multiple workflow run steps in one action.

Once you are done reading this section, you will be able to create a **composite run steps** action and verify that it works as intended by using it in a workflow.

Prerequisites

To follow the steps presented in this section, you will need the following:

1. A new GitHub repository. Throughout this section, the `talktopri/a-composite-run-steps-action` repository will be used.

2. A local copy of your GitHub repository. Use the `git clone` command to clone your GitHub repository to your workstation. Revisit *Chapter 1, Learning the Foundations for GitHub Actions,* if you need more details on how to accomplish that.

3. The action created in this section creates an npm test and builds a workflow. For this reason, you will need to have `Node.js` version 12.x or later installed on your workstation.

4. A `package.json` file. Once you have `Node.js` installed on your workstation, open a shell window and, from within your GitHub repository directory, type `npm init -y` to initialize the directory, accepting all of its default values.

> **Important note**
> To download `Node.js`, visit `https://nodejs.org/en/download/current/`.

The following screenshot shows a GitHub repository being cloned locally. Note how the `cd` command changed the directory from `Desktop` to the `/Desktop/a-composite-run-steps-action` repository directory. Then, the `package.json` file was generated once `npm init -y` was executed:

```
testesdapri ~/Desktop: $ git clone https://github.com/testesdapri/a-composite-run-steps-action.git
Cloning into 'a-composite-run-steps-action'...
remote: Enumerating objects: 11, done.
remote: Counting objects: 100% (11/11), done.
remote: Compressing objects: 100% (8/8), done.
remote: Total 11 (delta 0), reused 0 (delta 0), pack-reused 0
Unpacking objects: 100% (11/11), done.
testesdapri ~/Desktop: $ cd a-composite-run-steps-action/
testesdapri ~/Desktop/a-composite-run-steps-action: $ npm init -y
Wrote to /Users/talktopri/Desktop/a-composite-run-steps-action/package.json:
```

Figure 5.11 – Cloning a GitHub repository and initializing a new npm package

The examples in this section simply print a string to the screen, as the following screenshot shows. If you are comfortable using Node.js, you might want to consider adding a test.js file to your repository, which will then be used during the workflow run:

Figure 5.12 – The test and build scripts are simple commands to output strings to the screen

Defining the action

Every action needs a metadata file. To start your **composite run steps** action, create a metadata file within your GitHub repository, as illustrated in the following code snippet. This file will define the main entry point, as well as any I/Os for your action. The metadata file can be called either action.yml or action.yaml:

```
name: "A simple action that will use npm to create a build and
run a test"


runs:
  using: "composite"
  steps:
    - run: npm ci
      shell: bash
    - run: npm run test
      shell: bash
    - run: npm run build
      shell: bash
```

Note how the metadata file uses many `run` steps within the same action. Also, notice that the `using: "composite"` key-value pair was added to specify the type of action being used.

Differently from the JavaScript action, the **composite run steps** action examples used in this section do not require another file to define the logic that the action itself will use. The next steps will be to simply create a workflow file, pass your action to it, and ensure all works as expected.

Ensuring all works as expected

You have written your first **composite run steps** action—well done! Now, you have the opportunity to add your action to a workflow file—similar to what you accomplished in previous chapters—to verify that your code works well.

To ensure your action works as expected, create a new workflow file in your GitHub repository. Remember that workflow files must live in the `/.github/workflows/` directory. If you need details on how to create a workflow file, visit *Chapter 2, Deep Diving into GitHub Actions*.

Next, paste the following content into your newly created workflow file. This will trigger a workflow run when a new `push` event happens. Notice how your newly created action is passed under `steps`:

```
name: npm test and build

on:
  push

jobs:
  build:
    runs-on: ubuntu-latest
    steps:
      - uses: actions/checkout@v2
      - uses: actions/setup-node@v2
        with:
          node-version: 14
      - uses: testesdapri/a-composite-run-steps-action@main
```

The push event that created the workflow file should already have triggered the action. To verify this, click on the **Actions** tab. Then, click on the most recent workflow run, if you have multiple workflow runs in that repository, and click on **action**. This will take you to the **Action run** page, where you will be able to see each step completing successfully, as illustrated in the following screenshot:

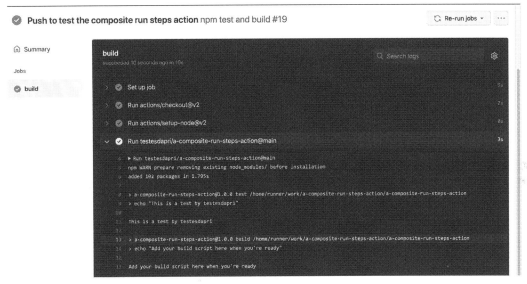

Figure 5.13 – Viewing the logs to validate that the composite run steps action ran successfully

Note how the `This is a test by testesdapri` and `Add your build script here when you're ready` strings, which were defined in the `package.json` file, are printed on the screen successfully.

Excellent job! The **composite run steps** action you created works as expected and all the jobs are completed successfully.

Summary

Well done! You have completed *Chapter 5, Writing Your Own Actions*. With the new skills you gained, you can distinguish the benefits of using Docker and JavaScript actions. You have learned details about the metadata syntax that must be part of any actions you may create. The last few sections of this chapter walked you through the creation of three different types of actions: JavaScript, Docker container, and composite run steps actions.

Now that you have learned how to create your own actions, you are ready to understand more about GitHub Marketplace and how you can share your actions with the community in the next *Chapter 6, Marketplace: Finding Existing Actions and Publishing Your Own*.

6
Marketplace – Finding Existing Actions and Publishing Your Own

You have learned so much! The knowledge you have gathered thus far will allow you to confidently use **GitHub Actions** to implement creative solutions that will help improve your **continuous integration/continuous deployment** (**CI/CD**) tasks and workflows.

In previous chapters, you had the chance to write workflow files to incorporate existing actions and, most recently, you had the experience of writing actions from scratch using JavaScript, Docker, and **composite run steps**—way to go!

Now, it is time to explore the next step in using GitHub Actions: connecting with and participating in the community of developers who use GitHub Actions. **GitHub Marketplace** allows anyone to publish paid or free GitHub applications and GitHub actions. This chapter will walk you through finding existing actions that you can incorporate into your workflow, as well as publishing actions that you have created and want to make available to the community.

To help you expand your knowledge of GitHub Marketplace, this chapter is organized into the following sections:

- Overview
- Finding existing actions
- Publishing your own actions
- Removing your action from GitHub Marketplace

By the end of this chapter, you will be able to search GitHub Marketplace for existing actions created by the community. You will also have a strong understanding of the best practices to prepare your own actions to be published. Lastly, you will have learned about the steps to publish your actions to GitHub Marketplace.

Technical requirements

In addition to the skills you have learned throughout previous chapters, you will need the following to successfully reproduce the steps presented in this chapter:

- A GitHub account
- An action that you have created in a public GitHub repository

Overview

By using **GitHub Marketplace**, you can find apps and actions within various categories such as CI, project management, code review, security, monitoring, and many others.

To access GitHub Marketplace and start browsing the many tools available, navigate to `https://github.com/marketplace`. This will take you to the following web page:

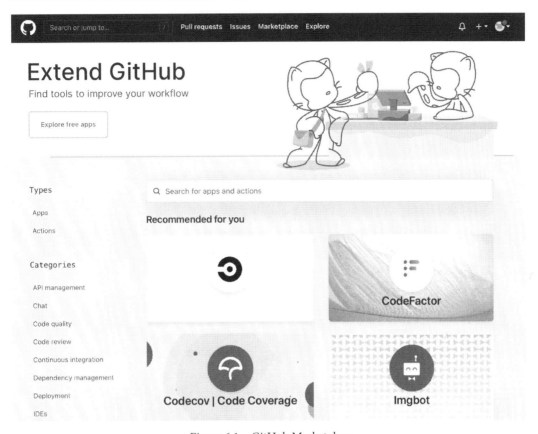

Figure 6.1 – GitHub Marketplace

While there are both paid and free apps in GitHub Marketplace, all GitHub actions are free.

GitHub Marketplace can be used both for publishing your own actions and finding existing ones. The next section will walk you through finding existing actions created and published by other GitHub Actions users.

Finding existing actions

As you have learned in previous chapters, using existing actions is a very efficient way to use GitHub Actions without the need to write the code for them. The GitHub Actions community is regularly contributing new actions to the GitHub Marketplace daily. There are over 7,000 actions that you can browse through, and it is likely that you will find something to help you with your CI/CD tasks.

Important note
You can browse GitHub Marketplace without being logged in to your GitHub user account. You will need to be logged in to add an existing action to your workflow, however.

The next steps will guide you in searching for actions within Marketplace:

1. To start browsing existing actions, navigate to `https://github.com/marketplace`.

2. Then, click on **Actions**, on the left-hand side.

   You can navigate the many pages of over 7,000 existing actions, or filter the results by category, such as **Continuous integration**, **Dependency management**, as illustrated in the following screenshot:

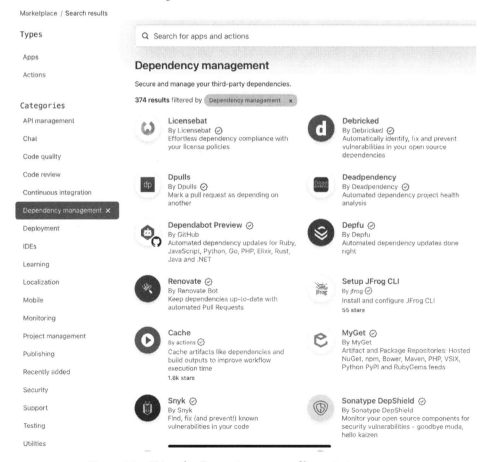

Figure 6.2 – Using the Categories menu to filter existing actions

Alternatively, you can use the search bar to type freely and search for an action.

Notice that many actions have a checkmark next to them. That is the **verified creator badge**, which means that GitHub has verified the creator of that action as a partner organization:

1. When you find an action that meets your workflow needs, click on it to be taken to the **Action** page. You can learn more about an action by reviewing its documentation, usage, prerequisites, and other details that the creator of that action made available.

2. Then, when you are ready to use that action, click on the **Use latest version** button on the right-hand side of the page. That button will include a drop-down option, if the action has more than one version available. This is illustrated in the following screenshot:

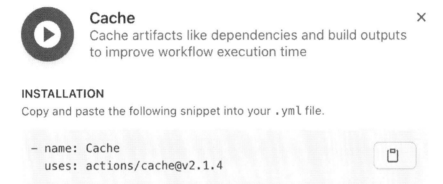

Figure 6.3 – The action's page and installation instructions

3. Lastly, review the installation instructions, which will explain how to add the action to your workflow. In many cases, incorporating an existing action is as easy as adding it to your workflow file, similar to what the many examples in *Chapter 3, A Closer Look at Workflows*, showed.

GitHub Marketplace is a rich resource to use when you are planning your CI/CD pipelines and workflows. By browsing it, you will likely find actions that can improve your code and provide inspiration to help you write your own actions.

Now that you have learned ways to search and find existing actions, it is time to learn how to leverage GitHub Marketplace to publish your own actions.

Publishing your own actions

In *Chapter 5, Writing Your Own Actions*, you learned how to write an action using JavaScript, Docker, and composite run steps. Sharing your actions is an excellent way to share your knowledge, as well as collaborating with and participating in the GitHub Actions community.

This section will introduce the prerequisites and steps you need to follow to successfully publish your own action to GitHub Marketplace.

Prerequisites

Before you can publish your action to GitHub Marketplace, you must meet the following prerequisites:

- Your action must live in a public GitHub repository.

- The repository must contain one single action.

- The action's metadata file—`action.yaml` or `action.yml`—must live in the root of the repository.

- The `name` value in the action metadata file must be unique. Therefore, it cannot match an existing action or a category in GitHub Marketplace. It also cannot match the name of a user or organization within GitHub, unless it is the user or organization publishing the action. Lastly, it cannot match the name of any GitHub feature.

By matching these requirements, your action will be immediately published to GitHub Marketplace, without the need for this to be reviewed by GitHub.

Assuming that your action meets these requirements, your next step will be to prepare your action to be published.

Preparing and publishing your action

This section will use the `testesdapri/a-docker-action` repository, created in *Chapter 5, Writing Your Own Actions*, as an example. Notice in the following screenshot how this repository's README file only contains the name of the repository and does not include any details about the action itself:

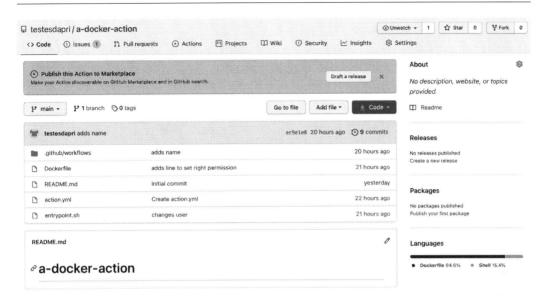

Figure 6.4 – A public Docker action

When other GitHub Marketplace users find your action, they will likely need to understand what your action does. To help them, edit the README file to include details such as the following:

- What your action does
- Required and optional **input and output (I/O)** arguments
- Secrets and environments the action uses
- An example to show how to use your action

The following contents were added to the README file of testesdapri/a-docker-action:

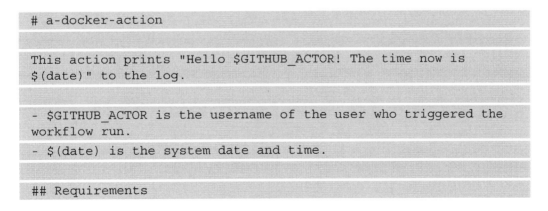

```
# a-docker-action

This action prints "Hello $GITHUB_ACTOR! The time now is
$(date)" to the log.

- $GITHUB_ACTOR is the username of the user who triggered the
workflow run.
- $(date) is the system date and time.

## Requirements
```

```
None. This action is simple, lightweight, and should work by
simply adding it to your workflow file

## Example usage

uses: testesdapri/a-docker-action@v1.0

Created with ♥ by @testesdapri
```

Next, you may want to consider adding a `branding` key to your `action.yml` file. This allows you to choose a color and icon for your GitHub action, which helps personalize and distinguish your action in GitHub Marketplace.

The following `branding` key was added to the `action.yml` file in the `testesdapri/a-docker-action` repository:

```
name: 'My Docker action'

description: 'Simply running a bash command and showing the
time it executed'

runs:
  using: 'docker'
  image: 'Dockerfile'

branding:
  icon: 'book'
  color: 'purple'
```

> **Important note**
>
> To learn more about all the icons and colors supported by GitHub, visit `https://docs.github.com/en/actions/creating-actions/metadata-syntax-for-github-actions#branding`.

Nice work in preparing your action to be published! You are ready to publish your action. To do that, proceed as follows:

1. Navigate to the main page of your GitHub repository. Notice the banner that says **Publish this Action to Marketplace**, as *Figure 6.4* shows. That banner was automatically added to your repository when you created the metadata file.

2. Click on **Draft a release**.

3. On the next page, click on the **accept the GitHub Marketplace Developer Agreement** link. Then, read the agreement terms, check the checkbox, and click on **Accept Terms**, as illustrated in the following screenshot:

GitHub Marketplace Developer Agreement v2.3   ✕

for longer than one month pursuant to 7(a);
- ○ iii. the Developer is in substantial or persistent breach of any warranties or representations under this Data Protection Addendum;
- ○ iv. the Developer is no longer carrying on business, is dissolved, enters receivership, or a winding up order is made on behalf of Developer.
- • c. Breach. Failure to comply with the provisions of this Data Protection Addendum is considered a material breach under the Master Services Agreement.
- • d. Notification.
  In the event that Developer determines that it can no longer meet its privacy obligations under this Agreement, it must notify GitHub immediately.
  In the event that Developer was certified under Privacy Shield and allows that certification to lapse or otherwise cannot remain certified under Privacy Shield, Developer must notify GitHub immediately.
- • e. Modifications. GitHub may modify this Addendum from time to time as required by law, with thirty days' notice to Developer. If Developer is unable to comply with the modifications to the Addendum, GitHub may terminate the Agreement.
- • f. Upon Termination, Developer must:
- ○ i. take reasonable and appropriate steps to stop processing of the Protected Data;
- ○ ii. within thirty days of termination, delete any Protected Data Developer stores on GitHub's behalf; and
- ○ iii. provide GitHub with reasonable assurance that Developer has stopped processing the Protected Data and deleted the stored Protected Data.
  A1-8. Liability for Data Processing

- • a. Direct Liability. Developer will be liable to GitHub for actual damages caused by any breach of this Addendum subject to the terms in Section 8, Limitation on Liability of the Marketplace Developer Agreement.

☑ By clicking "Accept Terms" below, you agree to the GitHub Marketplace Developer Agreement v2.3 on behalf of ⬛ testesdapri

[Accept Terms]

Figure 6.5 – Accepting the GitHub Marketplace Developer Agreement

4. You may be asked to set up **two-factor authentication (2FA)** before you can check the **Publish this release to the GitHub Marketplace** checkbox. If so, follow the prompts to set up 2FA. Then, navigate to your repository's main page again, and click on **Draft a Release** again.

5. Select a primary category that applies to your action. You may also want to select a secondary category.

6. Then, add the tag version and a title for the release, as illustrated in the following screenshot. When all looks good, click on **Publish release**:

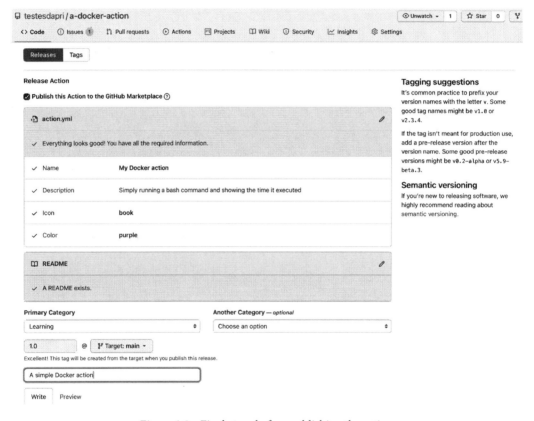

Figure 6.6 – Final steps before publishing the action

You will be taken to your repository's **Releases** page, where you can verify that your action has been published to GitHub Marketplace. In the following screenshot, notice the **Marketplace** badge:

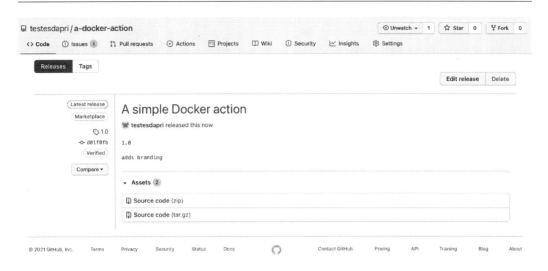

Figure 6.7 – The Releases page shows the Marketplace badge

Click on the **Marketplace** badge to be taken to the **Actions** page in GitHub Marketplace. Alternatively, you can navigate to `https://github.com/marketplace/actions/<your-action>`, where `<your-action>` should be replaced by the name of your action, as illustrated in the following screenshot:

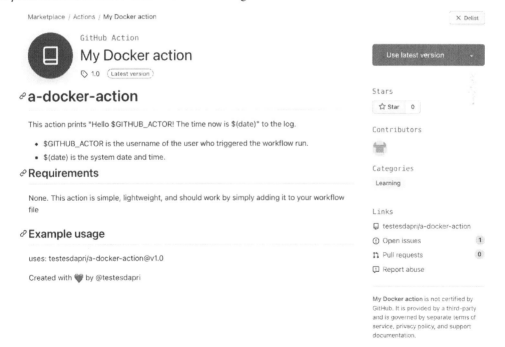

Figure 6.8 – Your action in GitHub Marketplace

Wonderful accomplishment! Your action has been successfully published to GitHub Marketplace—well done! Other GitHub users will now be able to add your action to their workflow files.

If you decide that you are not ready to keep your action available in GitHub Marketplace, you can remove it. The next section will provide the steps to accomplish that.

Removing your action from GitHub Marketplace

You can remove an action that has been published on GitHub Marketplace. To do that, follow these steps:

1. Navigate to the main page of the GitHub repository where your action lives.

2. Click **Releases**, on the right-hand side of the page. This will take you to your repository's **Releases** page, the page that *Figure 6.7* shows.

3. On the **Releases** page, click on **Edit**, as illustrated in the following screenshot:

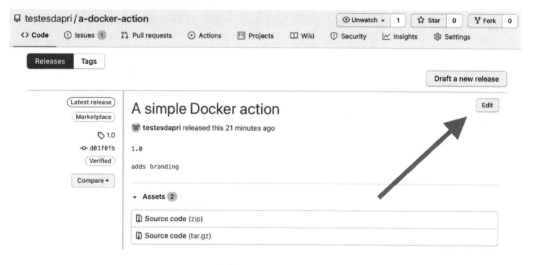

Figure 6.9 – Clicking Edit on the Releases page

4. Then, uncheck the **Publish this Action to the GitHub Marketplace** checkbox and click on **Update release**, as illustrated in the following screenshot:

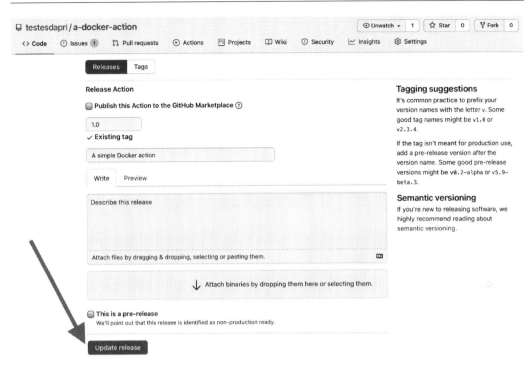

Figure 6.10 – Clicking Update release will remove the action from GitHub Marketplace

Good job! Your action has been successfully removed from GitHub Marketplace.

Summary

Excellent work! You have reached the end of *Chapter 6, Marketplace: Finding Existing Actions and Publishing Your Own*. You are one step closer to completing this book and growing your knowledge of GitHub Actions.

By reading this chapter, you have gained the experience needed to navigate around GitHub Marketplace and search for actions created by the community. You reviewed best practices to help you prepare your repository before publishing your action. You followed the steps to successfully publish your action in GitHub Marketplace and, lastly, you learned how to remove your action as well.

You have accomplished an important milestone: you now know how to start using GitHub Actions to implement or optimize your CI/CD workflows and your DevOps practices! Use this expertise to plan and execute a wide variety of workflows that can integrate with other platforms you already use. Use your creativity to write actions that can be as simple or as complex as you need them to be—the sky is the limit!

The more you use GitHub Actions and practice your newly gained skills, the more proficient you will be. Over time, you will be using GitHub Actions in most of your CI/CD, DevOps, and general automation workflows. For this reason, the next *Chapter 7, Migrations* will show you the steps needed to migrate from other platforms such as GitLab, Azure Pipelines, and CircleCI to GitHub Actions.

Section 3: Customizing Existing Actions, Migrations, and the Future of GitHub Actions

Section 3 will teach you that not all GitHub actions need to be created from scratch. Because Actions is open source, the user has access to actions created by the community. *Section 3* will also help users who are interested in migrating from their current solutions (such as GitLab, Jenkins, and Azure DevOps) to GitHub Actions. Finally, you will receive insights into what you can do with the skills learned from the book, and what the future of GitHub Actions looks like.

The following chapters will be covered in this section:

- *Chapter 7, Migrations*
- *Chapter 8, Contributing to the Community and Finding Help*
- *Chapter 9, The Future of GitHub Actions*

7
Migrations

As you learned in *Chapter 1*, *Learning the Foundations for GitHub Actions*, **Continuous Integration and Continuous Delivery (CI/CD)** practices became popular and were integrated as part of the software development life cycle years before GitHub Actions was launched. Other platforms such as **Azure Pipelines**, **GitLab**, and **Jenkins** were used to create automated pipelines that could integrate with the code hosted on GitHub.

You have learned that GitHub Actions allows you to create powerful and highly customized **CI/CD** workflows, with the added convenience of using the same platform where your code is hosted. As you continue evaluating and learning more about GitHub Actions, you will probably start thinking about the benefits of migrating your existing pipelines to GitHub Actions.

This chapter will walk you through the process of migrating CI/CD pipelines from Azure Pipelines, GitLab, and Jenkins to GitHub. By reading this chapter, you will learn about the similarities between these platforms and how the different migration processes can be made very simple.

This chapter is organized into three main sections, which can be read in any order, to help you create a migration plan that best fits your needs:

- Considerations before you migrate
- Migrating from Azure Pipelines
- Migrating from GitLab CI/CD
- Migrating from Jenkins

By the end of this chapter, you will have gathered the skills and knowledge you need to migrate your existing CI/CD pipelines from other platforms to GitHub Actions.

Technical requirements

In addition to the skills you learned in previous chapters, you will need an account with the appropriate access permissions to make changes to your existing Azure, GitLab, or Jenkins configuration.

You will also need to create a repository on GitHub where you can migrate your workflow files to. To review the steps to create a GitHub repository, read *Chapter 1, Learning the Foundations for GitHub Actions*.

Considerations before you migrate

Migrations can be a complex and disruptive task. Whether the migration you perform will potentially impact only your work, or your whole team's, consider carefully planning the migration steps ahead of time. This section outlines the best practices that you can use to support your migration plans and set you up for success.

Before you start migrating your CI/CD workflows and tasks, consider the following preparatory steps:

1. **Timeline**: When is the migration slated to begin and be completed? Setting a timeline to complete your migration is a good first step to help prepare you and your team. By defining a timeline of events for the migration process, you can also prioritize which tasks need to be completed first.

2. **Learn the steps that need to be followed**: Take advantage of learning materials such as this book and your platforms' public documentation to learn what migration steps you need to follow. Familiarize yourself with potential incompatibilities between platforms and possible workarounds.

3. **Do a test run**: Before migrating any production workflows or code, test the planned steps using code or environment variables that will not cause problems in case something doesn't go to plan (that is, a testing environment). Take comprehensive notes during your test run, which can be helpful during the production migration.

4. **Consider dependencies**: If your workflow integrates with other platforms or has other dependencies, such as specific software or versions, take those into consideration when you are planning the migration steps.

5. **Communicate with teams and individuals that might be impacted by the migration**: Send notifications ahead of the migration date to allow teams and individuals to prepare ahead of time. Consider sending alerts, emails, or notifications before starting the migration and once it has been completed.

6. **Test that everything works as expected**: After all of the workflows have been migrated, run tests to ensure all functionalities are working as expected.

Once you feel confident that your migration plan is in a healthy state and your tests have run successfully, start the migration.

The next section will introduce the key concepts you need to learn to migrate your CI/CD workflows from Azure Pipelines to GitHub Actions.

Migrating from Azure Pipelines

You have studied and compared the features and benefits of both Azure Pipelines and GitHub Actions, and you have decided to migrate some, or all, of your workflows to GitHub Actions. The next few sections will introduce basic steps to help you perform this migration successfully.

To get started with the migration, follow these steps:

1. Migrate your code to GitHub. If your code is not hosted on GitHub already, create a new repository and push your code there. Please refer to *Chapter 1, Learning the Foundations for GitHub Actions*, and review the steps to accomplish that.

2. Read the documentation to learn more about the workflow configuration and syntax differences between both platforms.

> **Important note**
> The comprehensive documentation to support the migration from Azure Pipelines to GitHub Actions can be found at `https://docs.github.com/en/actions/learn-github-actions/migrating-from-azure-pipelines-to-github-actions`.

3. Start migrating the contents of your `azure-pipelines.yml` file to a GitHub repository.

Syntax differences

There are many similarities between Azure Pipelines and GitHub Actions. For example, YAML is used to write the workflow configuration file on both platforms. There are, however, a few syntax differences that you must be aware of when migrating your workflow configuration file from Azure Pipelines to GitHub Actions.

The following list will illustrate the main differences in vocabulary and syntax between Azure Pipelines and GitHub Actions.

Pipeline versus workflow

GitHub Actions defines a **workflow** as an automated procedure that can be used to build, test, deploy, release, or package a project. **Pipelines** are equivalent to **workflows** on Azure Pipelines.

script versus run

The `script` key is used in Azure Pipelines to run the code as a step using a command-line tool such as Bash or PowerShell. It is equivalent to the `run` key used in GitHub Actions.

trigger versus on

Azure Pipelines uses `trigger` as the key to define the event that will trigger the pipeline to run. It is equivalent to the `on` key, which GitHub Actions uses to define the event that will trigger the workflow to run.

pool

Azure Pipelines uses the `pool` key to manage the pool of agents, or machines, where the job will be run.

Default shell

The default shell for scripts to run when using a Windows platform in Azure Pipelines is the **Command shell**. GitHub Actions' default shell for scripts running on Windows platforms is PowerShell.

vmImage versus runs-on

Azure Pipelines uses the `vmImage` key, which, similarly to the `runs-on` key used in GitHub Actions, defines what operating system will be used on the host machine.

task versus uses

Azure Pipelines uses the `task` key, which is similar to the GitHub Actions `uses` key. Both of these keys bring blocks of code that are often built by the community, such as **actions**, into a pipeline or workflow file.

displayName versus name

Azure Pipelines uses `displayName` to give each step a friendly name that will be displayed on the user interface. It is similar to the `name` key used in GitHub Actions.

Now that you have learned more about the syntax differences between Azure Pipelines and GitHub Actions, you are ready to review how a pipeline file can be migrated to a GitHub Actions workflow file.

The following screenshot shows a simple `YAML` file in Azure Pipelines. This pipeline will be triggered by **push** events against the `main` branch, creating an Ubuntu virtual machine where `Node.js` will be installed and the build will be created:

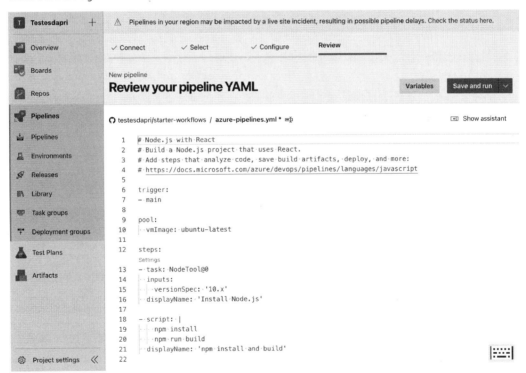

Figure 7.1 – A YAML file in Azure Pipelines

Considering the syntax comparison you learned about previously, you can simply migrate an Azure Pipelines YAML file to GitHub and, by adjusting a few keys, create a GitHub Actions workflow that looks like this:

```
name: Node.js CI

on:
  push:
    branches: [ main ]

jobs:
  build-on-linux:
    runs-on: ubuntu-latest
    steps:
    - uses: actions/checkout@v2

    - name: Setup Node.js environment
      uses: actions/setup-node@v2
      with:
        node-version: 12

    - name: Install Node.js modules
      run: npm install

    - name: Create build
      run: npm run build
```

While the examples in this section will help you get started with your migration from Azure Pipelines to GitHub Actions, they do not present a comprehensive list of the distinctions between both tools. Consider researching, studying, and cross-referencing the documentation of both Azure Pipelines and GitHub Actions, which will uncover other important differences in the syntax used by both platforms.

Next, we will learn more about migrating automated tasks from GitLab CI/CD.

Migrating from GitLab CI/CD

You have studied and compared the features and benefits of both GitLab CI/CD and GitHub Actions, and you have decided to migrate some, or all, of your workflows to GitHub Actions. The next few sections will introduce basic steps to help you perform this migration successfully.

To get started with the migration, follow these steps:

1. Migrate your code to GitHub. If your code is not hosted on GitHub already, create a new repository and push your code there. Please refer to *Chapter 1*, *Learning the Foundations for GitHub Actions*, and review the steps to accomplish that.

2. Read the documentation to learn more about the workflow configuration and syntax differences between both platforms.

> **Important note**
>
> The comprehensive documentation to support the migration from GitLab CI/CD to GitHub Actions can be found at `https://docs.github.com/en/actions/learn-github-actions/migrating-from-gitlab-cicd-to-github-actions`.

3. Start migrating the contents of your `.gitlab-ci.yml` file to a GitHub repository.

Syntax differences

There are many similarities between GitLab CI/CD and GitHub Actions. For example, YAML is used to write the workflow configuration file on both platforms. There are, however, a few syntax differences that you must be aware of when migrating your workflow configuration file from GitLab CI/CD to GitHub Actions.

The following list will illustrate the main differences in vocabulary and syntax between GitLab CI/CD and GitHub Actions.

Pipeline versus workflow

GitHub Actions defines a **workflow** as an automated procedure that can be used to build, test, deploy, release, or package a project. **Pipelines** are equivalent to **workflows** on GitLab CI/CD.

GitLab CI/CD also uses `workflow` as a key within the YAML file to determine whether a pipeline should be created.

script versus run

The `script` key is used in GitLab CI/CD to run code as a step using a command-line tool such as Bash or PowerShell. It is equivalent to the `run` key used in GitHub Actions.

stage versus needs

GitLab CI/CD uses the `stages` key. Jobs within the same `stage` key will run in parallel, but a job in a different `stage` key will not run until the jobs in the prior `stage` key are completed. The equivalent key in GitHub Actions is `needs`.

Docker images

While both GitLab CI/CD and GitHub Actions support running jobs in a Docker image, the keys used in the YAML file are different. GitLab CI/CD uses the `image` key to define Docker images, and GitHub Actions uses the `container` key.

rules versus if

GitHub Actions uses one simple `if` key to prevent a job from running unless a specific condition is met. GitLab CI/CD uses the `rules` key and the conditional `if` key.

> **Important note**
>
> GitLab CI/CD's feature for scheduling workflows is configured using the user interface. In comparison, you can use the `on` key within a GitHub Actions workflow file to schedule a **cron job** to determine when a job should run. Keep this in mind when migrating a pipeline from GitLab CI/CD to GitHub Actions that needs to run on a set schedule.

Now that you have learned more about the syntax differences between GitLab CI/CD and GitHub Actions, you are ready to review how a pipeline file can be migrated to a GitHub Actions workflow file.

The following screenshot shows a simple YAML file in GitLab CI/CD. This pipeline will be triggered by **push** events against the `master` branch, triggering a few different jobs. The jobs that are parts of the same stage, such as **test-job1** and **test-job2**, will run in parallel. All jobs will run commands that will print messages to the screen as they are completed successfully:

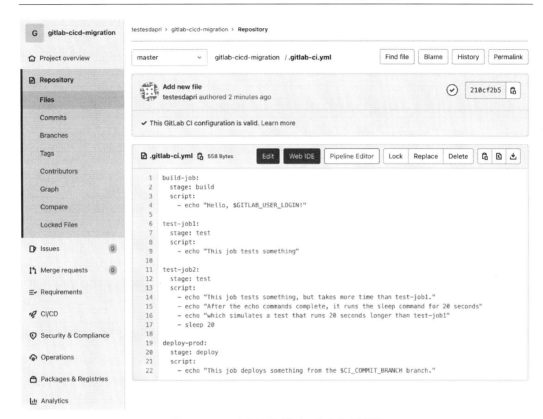

Figure 7.2 – A YAML file in GitLab CI/CD

Considering the syntax comparison you read previously, you can simply migrate a GitLab CI/CD YAML file to GitHub and, by adjusting a few keys, create a GitHub Actions workflow that looks like this:

```
name: GitLab CI/CD test

on:
  push:
    branches: [ main ]

jobs:
  build:
    runs-on: ubuntu-latest
    steps:
      - name: Run build command
      - run: echo "Hello $GITHUB_ACTOR!"
```

```
test-job1:
    runs-on: windows-latest
    steps:
    - name: Run test1
    - run: echo "This job tests something"

test-job2:
    runs-on: windows-latest
    steps:
    - name: Run test2
      run: echo "This job tests something, but takes more time
than test-job1."
      - run: echo "After the echo commands complete, it runs the
sleep command for 20 seconds"
      - run: echo "which simulates a test that runs 20 seconds
longer than job-test1."
      - run: sleep 20

deploy-prod:
    runs-on: windows-latest
    needs: [test-job1,test-job2]
    steps:
      - run: echo "This job deploys something new after the other
jobs complete"
```

While the examples in this section will help you get started with your migration from GitLab CI/CD to GitHub Actions, they do not present a comprehensive list of the distinctions between both tools. Consider researching, studying, and cross-referencing the documentation of both GitLab CI/CD and GitHub Actions, which will uncover other important differences in the syntax used by both platforms.

Next, we will learn more about migrating automated tasks from Jenkins.

Migrating from Jenkins

You have studied and compared the features and benefits of both Jenkins and GitHub Actions, and you have decided to migrate some, or all, of your workflows to GitHub Actions. The next few sections will introduce basic steps to help you perform this migration successfully.

To get started with the migration, follow these steps:

1. Migrate your code to GitHub. If your code is not hosted on GitHub already, create a new repository and push your code there. Please refer to *Chapter 1, Learning the Foundations for GitHub Actions*, and review the steps to accomplish that.

2. Read the documentation to learn more about the workflow configuration and syntax differences between both platforms.

> **Important note**
> The comprehensive documentation to support the migration from Jenkins to GitHub Actions can be found at `https://docs.github.com/en/actions/learn-github-actions/migrating-from-jenkins-to-github-actions`.

3. Start migrating the contents of your **Jenkins pipeline script** to a GitHub repository.

Syntax differences

As you have learned, GitHub Actions workflows are written using YAML. In comparison, Jenkins Pipelines scripts can be written using either **Declarative Pipeline** syntax or **Scripted Pipeline** syntax. Only Declarative Pipeline syntax will be covered in this book, given its simplicity and recentness.

Declarative Pipeline and YAML share many similarities. There are, however, a few syntax differences that you must be aware of when migrating your Jenkins script written using Directive Pipeline syntax to a GitHub Actions workflow file.

To help you plan the migration, the following list will illustrate a few differences in vocabulary and syntax between Jenkins and GitHub Actions.

Agent versus runners

Jenkins uses an **agent** in a similar way to how GitHub Actions uses **runners**. They specify the environment where the pipeline will be executed and represent a required key that must be added to the pipeline script—the same way runners are required in a GitHub Actions workflow. Because Jenkins deployments are usually self-hosted, you might want to consider using GitHub Actions self-hosted runners to keep a similar deployment strategy during the migration. Please refer to *Chapter 4, Working with Self-Hosted Runners*, to review what self-hosted runners are and how to use them.

Stages versus jobs

As you have seen, GitHub Actions use **jobs** to define a set of steps that will be executed on the same runner. Jenkins' Directive Pipeline has similar functionality, which is defined by the **stages** directive in the script.

Tools versus self-runner specifications

Although this is not a required directive, Jenkins uses **tools** to define what software must be installed on the agent. This is similar to the set of preinstalled software that is available with GitHub-hosted runners.

Now that you have learned more about the syntax differences between Jenkins and GitHub Actions, you are ready to review how a pipeline file can be migrated to a GitHub Actions workflow file.

The following screenshot shows a sample script using Maven in Jenkins. This pipeline will install Maven, leverage code from a GitHub repository, run Maven on a Unix agent, record the results, and archive the artifact:

```
1 ▾  pipeline {
2        agent any
3
4 ▾      tools {
5            // Install the Maven version configured as "M3" and add it to the path.
6            maven "M3"
7        }
8
9 ▾      stages {
10 ▾         stage('Build') {
11 ▾             steps {
12                    // Get some code from a GitHub repository
13                    git 'https://github.com/jglick/simple-maven-project-with-tests.git'
14
15                    // Run Maven on a Unix agent.
16                    sh "mvn -Dmaven.test.failure.ignore=true clean package"
17
18                    // To run Maven on a Windows agent, use
19                    // bat "mvn -Dmaven.test.failure.ignore=true clean package"
20                }
21
22 ▾             post {
23                    // If Maven was able to run the tests, even if some of the test
24                    // failed, record the test results and archive the jar file.
25 ▾                 success {
26                        junit '**/target/surefire-reports/TEST-*.xml'
27                        archiveArtifacts 'target/*.jar'
28                    }
29                }
30            }
31        }
32  }
```

Figure 7.3 – A Directive Pipeline sample script in Jenkins

Considering the syntax comparison you read previously, you can migrate a script written using Directive Pipeline in Jenkins to GitHub and, by adjusting a few keys, create a GitHub Actions workflow that looks like this:

```
name: Java CI with Maven


on: workflow_dispatch


jobs:
  build-jdk11:
    runs-on: ubuntu-latest
    steps:
    - name: Set up JDK 11
      uses: actions/checkout@v2
```

```
    - uses: actions/setup-java@v2
      with:
        java-version: 11
        distribution: 'adopt'

    - name: Build with Maven
      run: mvn -B clean package --file pom.xml

    - name: archive-artifacts
      run: |
          mvn --batch-mode --update-snapshots verify
          mkdir staging && cp target/*.jar staging

    - name: upload package
      uses: actions/upload-artifact@v2
      with:
        name: Package
        path: staging
```

While the examples in this section will help you get started with your migration from Jenkins to GitHub Actions, they do not present a comprehensive list of the distinctions between both tools. Consider researching, studying, and cross-referencing the documentation of both Jenkins and GitHub Actions, which will uncover other important differences in the syntax that is used by both platforms.

You have reached the end of this chapter: excellent job! You now know how to start planning and executing the migration of your CI/CD pipelines from platforms such as Gitlab CI/CD, Azure Pipelines, and Jenkins to GitHub Actions.

Summary

By reading the first seven chapters of this book, you have gathered the necessary skills to implement a complete CI/CD pipeline to automate important tasks that are part of your software development life cycle. You have also learned how to migrate your current pipelines and workflows from other platforms into GitHub Actions, which allows you to manage your code and automation in one single place.

As you begin to put these new skills into practice, you will likely have questions and require practical guidance. You will probably also want to share the lessons you have learned with others and appreciate being part of the community that makes GitHub Actions such a collaborative tool.

In the next *Chapter 8, Contributing to the Community and Finding Help*, you will review the resources available to support you in your journey of automating workflows with GitHub actions. You will also explore ways in which you can contribute to the community and find help when you need it.

8
Contributing to the Community and Finding Help

The best part of learning a new skill is putting it into practice. By reading the previous chapters, you gathered skills that will allow you to explore the many benefits of using GitHub Actions. You are now ready to design and implement a CI/CD pipeline that easily integrates your code with many tools! Continue learning about GitHub Actions by practicing it: use the examples you have seen throughout this book and adapt them to your own workflows and tasks.

As you continue developing your skills, keep the GitHub Actions community in mind. By interacting with a global group of people interested in using and improving GitHub Actions, you will be able to collaborate with the community, find help, share your knowledge, and continue learning.

By reading this chapter, you will learn about the many different ways in which you can collaborate with the GitHub Actions community, as well as with the GitHub Support team. To help explore the many platforms where you can both find help and contribute, this chapter is organized into the following sections:

- Hands-on learning

- Interacting with the GitHub Actions community

- Helping to improve GitHub Actions

- Requesting technical support

By the end of this chapter, you will feel comfortable finding the guidance and support to help you use GitHub Actions successfully. You will be able to take on the journey of exploring GitHub Actions in a way that fits your needs, while keeping a rich list of resources to review, both to find help and to share the lessons you will learn with others.

Technical requirements

In addition to the skills you have learned in previous chapters, you will need to use your GitHub user account to access some of the resources shared throughout this chapter.

Hands-on learning

You have seen, and hopefully practiced, many scenarios throughout this book where GitHub Actions were applied. Practice can be one of the most efficient ways of learning a new skill or technology. While the skills you have gathered by reading this book set you up to build successful workflows, you should not stop your learning journey here! GitHub provides an open source tool that you can leverage to continue learning other ways in which GitHub Actions and other GitHub features can be used: the GitHub Learning Lab.

The GitHub Learning Lab allows you to develop your skills by completing guided, lively, fun, and interactive projects. You can find individual courses or **learning paths**, which groups many courses that relate to a specific topic or technology.

> **Important note**
> To access the GitHub Learning Lab and see all the available courses, navigate to `https://lab.github.com`.

The GitHub Actions learning path includes 10 different courses. To see and complete all the available courses that are part of this path, follow these steps:

1. Navigate to `https://lab.github.com/githubtraining/devops-with-github-actions`.

2. Click on **Start free course**:

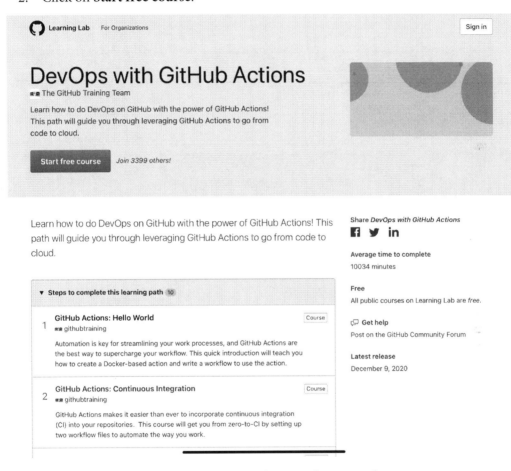

Figure 8.1 – The GitHub Actions learning path

3. Next, sign in using your GitHub user account credentials.

4. On the next screen, select the type of repository you prefer and click **Begin DevOps with GitHub Actions**. Note that you will need to be on the GitHub Pro plan if you decide to use a private repository:

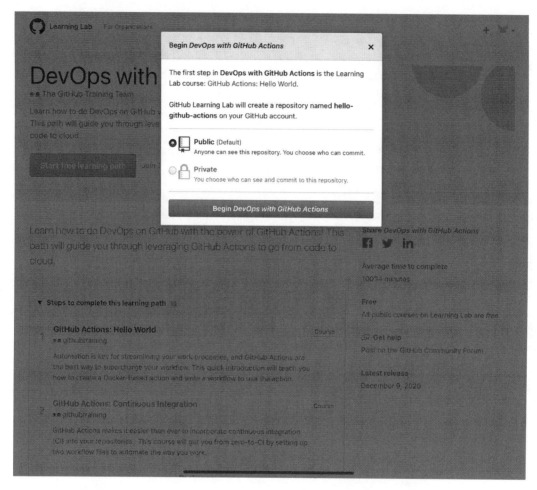

Figure 8.2 – Starting the DevOps with GitHub Actions learning path

5. The prompts in the next few screens will guide you in completing the tasks and projects within each course. Once you complete a course, you will be taken to the next one in the path, until you complete the full learning path. You can also start individual courses in any order that you prefer.

The GitHub Learning Lab is a great tool to keep in mind if you need a practical refresher, or if you would like to share additional resources with peers and friends.

Sharing the skills you have learned and participating in conversations with other members of the community can be a valuable way of keeping your skills current and improving GitHub Actions as a product.

Interacting with the GitHub Actions community

The GitHub community forum is the place where many GitHub users ask each other questions, interact with GitHub staff, and share knowledge and best practices. There are over 251 thousand posts concerning many different topics related to GitHub and its products, including GitHub Actions.

Consider the GitHub community forum your place to learn from and participate in existing posts, create new topics or questions, and help other fellow users by sharing your experience and knowledge. Using the GitHub community forum is free, and all you need is your GitHub user account.

GitHub Actions is one of the hottest topics in the GitHub community forum. It is not uncommon to see discussions created by the GitHub Actions product team, where they ask the community for their insight and opinions.

> **Important note**
> To visit the GitHub community forum, navigate to `https://github.community`.

Before you start interacting in the GitHub community forum, consider reviewing their code of conduct, located at `https://github.community/t/code-of-conduct/49`.

To start interacting with the GitHub Actions community in the GitHub community forum, follow these instructions:

1. Navigate to `https://github.community/c/code-to-cloud/github-actions/41`.

2. Log in. While it is not required that you log in to browse topics or conversations, you will need to log in using your GitHub user account credentials to create a new topic or reply on an existing one. To log in, click on **Log In** in the top right-hand corner:

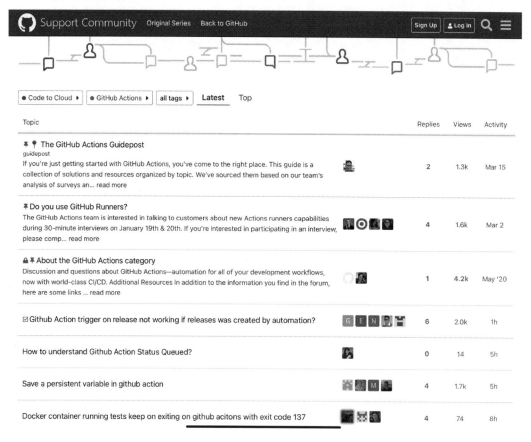

Figure 8.3 – The GitHub Actions topics in the GitHub community forum

3. Once you log in, you will be able to do the following:

- Create new topics.

- Add replies to, upvote, share, or bookmark topics.

- Configure notifications for specific topics:

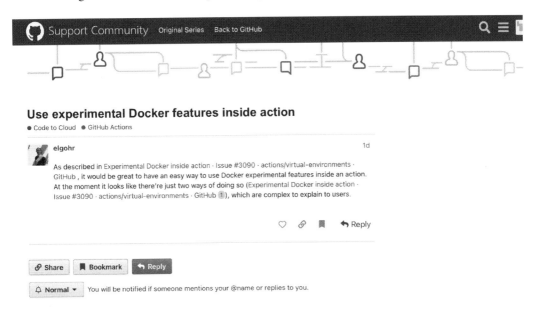

Figure 8.4 – The options available for a logged-in user

To create a new topic to ask for help, raise a feature request, or share something with the community, navigate to `https://github.community/new`, or click the **New Topic** button on any GitHub community forum page, once you have authenticated with your GitHub user account credentials:

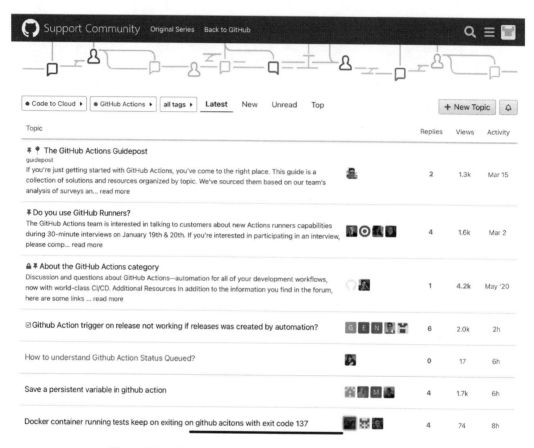

Figure 8.5 – Creating a new topic is as easy as pushing a button

You are now ready to be an active member of the GitHub Actions community! Make sure to visit the GitHub community forum regularly to learn what the community has been working on and contribute your own projects.

The open source nature of GitHub Actions makes it easy to both interact with the community and contribute with code, by raising GitHub issues and pull requests. The next section will introduce the GitHub Actions organization hosted on GitHub, and the many repositories you can contribute to.

Helping to improve GitHub Actions

As you become more familiar with GitHub Actions, you may find ways in which you can contribute your knowledge to improve the product itself. You can share your ideas and contributions by raising a feature request in the GitHub community forum, or by using the many public GitHub Actions repositories to report bugs and create pull requests with your code:

> **Important note**
> To access the GitHub Actions public repositories, visit `https://github.com/actions`.

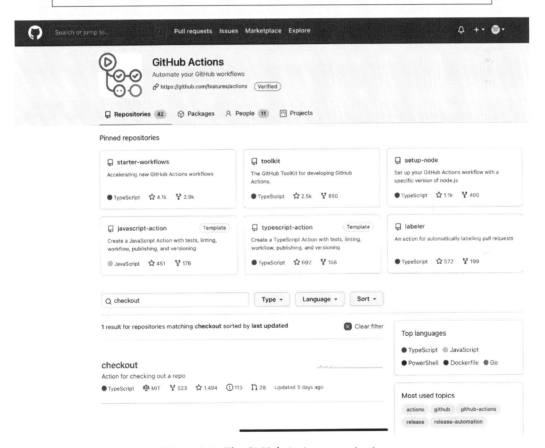

Figure 8.6 – The GitHub Actions organization

The GitHub Actions product team created an organization on GitHub that hosts many public repositories that the community has access to and can contribute to. Many of those repositories host some of the most commonly used actions, such as `actions/checkout`, used in some of the examples in *Chapter 3, A Closer Look at Workflows*.

Using the **GitHub Actions Toolkit** repository as an example, follow these steps to contribute to a public GitHub Actions repository:

1. Navigate to the repository main page, in this case, `https://github.com/actions/toolkit`.

2. Review the repository's `README` file, which also includes instructions on how to contribute to that project.

3. Create an issue to raise a feature request or bug report. Alternatively, create a branch, add your code, and propose changes by raising a pull request. If you need a refresher on how to accomplish this, review *Chapter 1, Learning the Foundations for GitHub Actions*:

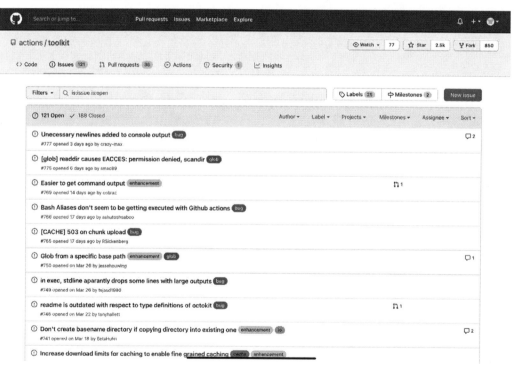

Figure 8.7 – GitHub Actions community members reporting bugs and requesting enhancements

You have learned how to help improve GitHub Actions by contributing code, reporting bugs, and requesting enhancements. The next section will introduce another resource for your GitHub Actions toolkit, GitHub Support, and how to reach out to them when things aren't going as well as you had hoped.

Requesting technical support

Although you have learned about many resources to help you get the best use out of GitHub Actions, sometimes, things may not work as expected. The GitHub Actions documentation and community may be able to help answer many questions, but sometimes, reaching out to technical support is the best solution.

GitHub Support can: help answer questions; troubleshoot issues that happened while you were using GitHub products; fix things that aren't working quite as they should; and help with feature requests and bug reports.

> **Important note**
>
> To request technical support, visit `https://support.github.com/contact`.

If you need to ask for help from GitHub Support, follow these steps:

1. Navigate to `https://support.github.com/contact`.
2. Sign in using your GitHub user account credentials.
3. Select the account your problem is related to.
4. Add a subject and a comprehensive description of the problem. In many cases, it is helpful to include a copy of the workflow file you are using, as well as any other details that can be helpful for the GitHub Support team in understanding and diagnosing the problem.

5.   Click **Send request**:

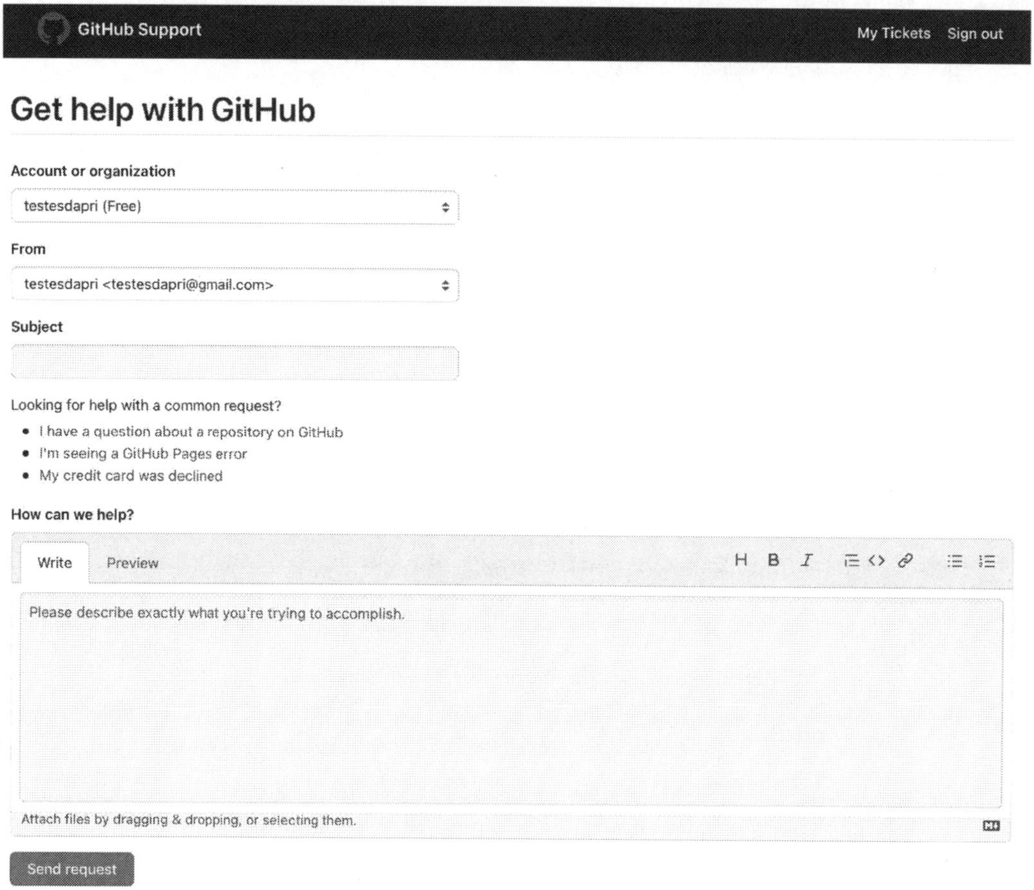

Figure 8.8 – Creating a support request

You will receive an email confirmation that your support ticket has been created, and somebody from the GitHub Support team will work with you via email.

Summary

Way to go! You have reached the end of *Chapter 8, Contributing to the Community and Finding Help*. You are now well equipped to venture into the exciting world of automating tasks and workflows using GitHub Actions. While you are exploring, creating, and learning, remember that you are not alone and that the GitHub Actions community is a powerful ally: collaborate, ask for help, read about their best practices, and share your findings as you go.

By finishing this chapter, you learned about the resources available to help you continue using GitHub Actions successfully. You can continue learning and practicing with the GitHub Learning Lab. You now know how to interact with the community in the GitHub community forum, and contribute code and ideas in the GitHub Actions public repositories. Finally, you reviewed the steps to reach out to GitHub Support when you need expert help. Don't forget the GitHub Actions documentation used throughout this book! You should revisit it often to feel more confident in your knowledge and skills

The community has a powerful influence on what new features and changes are added to GitHub Actions. You know how to find the hottest topics that the community is talking about and is interested in. In the next *Chapter 9, The Future of GitHub Actions*, you will learn about ways to stay in the know and keep up with what the future of GitHub Actions holds.

9
The Future of GitHub Actions

Soon, GitHub Actions will become an essential part of your CI/CD pipeline, no matter how simple or complex it may be. Given its importance in your workflow and tasks, you should always take advantage of updates and improvements that will continue improving GitHub Actions.

By reading this chapter, you will learn about resources that will help you stay up to date with the latest news and updates to GitHub Actions. To present those resources, this chapter is organized into the following sections:

- Checking the GitHub roadmap
- Reading the GitHub blog and changelog
- Connecting through social media

By the end of this chapter, you will know what social media accounts to follow and what pages to visit to learn about features and updates being added to GitHub Actions.

Technical requirements

You will need access to a device that has a connection to the internet.

Checking the GitHub roadmap

GitHub's roadmap is one of the most reliable ways to be informed about what the company is working on and plans on releasing in future months. The roadmap displays the release plans for many GitHub products, including GitHub Actions.

> **Important note**
>
> To see GitHub's roadmap, visit `https://github.com/github/roadmap/projects/1`.

The roadmap is organized into quarters. Each feature on the roadmap is categorized based on a few factors:

- **Feature area**: Such as **ecosystem**, which includes API features, for example, and **code-to-cloud**, which includes GitHub Actions.

- **Release phase**: Such as **alpha**, **beta**, and **generally available (GA)**.

- **Feature**: Such as **actions**, **docs**, **packages**, or **pages**.

- **Product SKU**: This represents the many GitHub product SKUs, such as GitHub team, GitHub Enterprise, GitHub AE, and others:

Figure 9.1 – The GitHub roadmap

Note how GitHub's roadmap lives in a public repository and was created using a GitHub feature called **Projects**. Within this project, all features represent GitHub issues. Because this is a repository, you can be notified when changes happen. To configure what kind of notification you want to receive, click on the **Notifications** button in the top right-hand corner and select your preferred option. If you would prefer not to receive any notifications, you can consider starring this repository, which won't send you notifications but can help you in navigating back to this repository at a later time. To star this repository, click on the **Star** button in the top right-hand corner.

To learn more about GitHub's roadmap, read the project's README file at https://github.com/github/roadmap/blob/main/README.md.

In addition to the roadmap, GitHub regularly announces new features, changes, and updates on their blog and changelog page.

Reading the GitHub blog and changelog

The GitHub blog is one of GitHub's many platforms to officially share announcements and updates. You will often see new blog posts from GitHub employees sharing news about the company, open source, community, and its products.

> **Important note**
>
> To access the GitHub blog, visit `https://github.blog/`. To view blog posts specifically about GitHub Actions, navigate to `https://github.blog/?s=GitHub%20Actions`.

The GitHub changelog is part of the GitHub blog and focuses on providing feature updates only. By visiting `https://github.blog/changelog/`, you will be able to see what changes were recently incorporated into GitHub products and features:

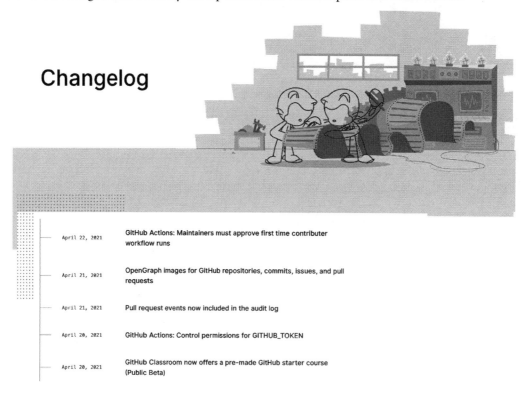

Figure 9.2 – The GitHub blog and changelog

GitHub is present on many different social media platforms, which they also use for important messages and announcements. The next section will help you find GitHub's social media accounts to help you not miss future announcements.

Connecting through social media

Historically, GitHub has made important announcements about new features or major updates to existing products during events such as Universe, their annual conference. GitHub is very active on social media, and often streams live events on platforms such as Twitch and YouTube. Consider connecting with GitHub's accounts to receive alerts when they go live or create a new post.

You can find GitHub on these platforms:

- Twitter, at `https://twitter.com/github`
- Youtube, at `https://www.youtube.com/github`
- Twitch, at `https://twitch.tv/github`
- LinkedIn, at `https://www.linkedin.com/company/github`
- Facebook, at `https://www.facebook.com/GitHub`:

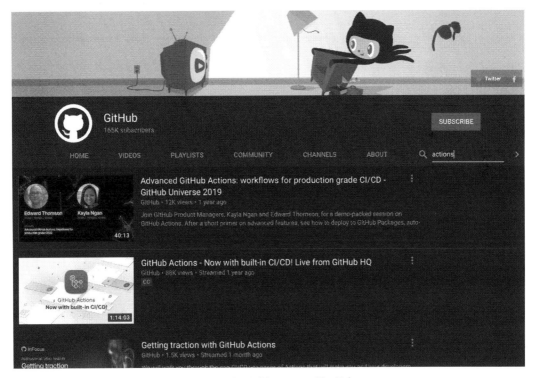

Fig. 9.3 – GitHub's page on YouTube

Summary

Outstanding work! You have reached the end of *Chapter 9, The Future of GitHub Actions,* and the end of *Automating Workflows with GitHub Actions.*

You are ready to put the new abilities you have gathered into practice. Now it is up to you to identify opportunities where your workflow can be improved and decluttered by implementing easy-to-write GitHub Actions workflows written in a simple YAML file, and that can accomplish so much. Remember to leverage GitHub Marketplace and find actions that fit your needs with little effort to implement. Deepen your knowledge by frequently visiting the GitHub documentation and interacting with the community. Automate repetitive tasks so that you can focus on what truly matters.

`Packt.com`

Subscribe to our online digital library for full access to over 7,000 books and videos, as well as industry leading tools to help you plan your personal development and advance your career. For more information, please visit our website.

Why subscribe?

- Spend less time learning and more time coding with practical eBooks and Videos from over 4,000 industry professionals

- Improve your learning with Skill Plans built especially for you

- Get a free eBook or video every month

- Fully searchable for easy access to vital information

- Copy and paste, print, and bookmark content

Did you know that Packt offers eBook versions of every book published, with PDF and ePub files available? You can upgrade to the eBook version at `packt.com` and as a print book customer, you are entitled to a discount on the eBook copy. Get in touch with us at `customercare@packtpub.com` for more details.

At `www.packt.com`, you can also read a collection of free technical articles, sign up for a range of free newsletters, and receive exclusive discounts and offers on Packt books and eBooks.

Other Books You May Enjoy

If you enjoyed this book, you may be interested in these other books by Packt:

Docker for Developers

Richard Bullington-McGuire, Andrew K. Dennis, and Michael Schwartz

ISBN: 978-1-78953-605-8

- Get up to speed with creating containers and understand how they work
- Package and deploy your containers to a variety of platforms
- Work with containers in the cloud and on the Kubernetes platform
- Deploy and then monitor the health and logs of running containers
- Explore best practices for working with containers from a security perspective
- Become familiar with scanning containers and using third-party security tools and libraries

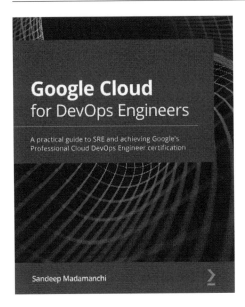

Google Cloud for DevOps Engineers

Sandeep Madamanchi

ISBN: 978-1-83921-801-9

- Categorize user journeys and explore different ways to measure SLIs
- Explore the four golden signals for monitoring a user-facing system
- Understand psychological safety along with other SRE cultural practices
- Create containers with build triggers and manual invocations
- Delve into Kubernetes workloads and potential deployment strategies
- Secure GKE clusters via private clusters, Binary Authorization, and shielded GKE nodes
- Get to grips with monitoring, Metrics Explorer, uptime checks, and alerting
- Discover how logs are ingested via the Cloud Logging API

Packt is searching for authors like you

If you're interested in becoming an author for Packt, please visit `authors.packtpub.com` and apply today. We have worked with thousands of developers and tech professionals, just like you, to help them share their insight with the global tech community. You can make a general application, apply for a specific hot topic that we are recruiting an author for, or submit your own idea.

Share Your Thoughts

Now you've finished *Automating Workflows with GitHub Actions*, we'd love to hear your thoughts! Scan the QR code below to go straight to the Amazon review page for this book and share your feedback or leave a review on the site that you purchased it from.

https://packt.link/r/1800560400

Your review is important to us and the tech community and will help us make sure we're delivering excellent quality content.

Index